# Memories of Dr Shinichi Suzuki

## Son of His Environment

### Lois Shepheard

Glass House Books
Brisbane

Lois bows to Dr Suzuki, as his secretary, Mitsuko Kawakami, looks on.

## About the Author

Australian violin and viola teacher and Suzuki teacher-trainer, Lois Shepheard, introduced the Suzuki Method to Victoria and established the Suzuki association, now called Suzuki Music (Victoria).

She is a graduate of the New South Wales State Conservatorium of Music and what is now known as the Talent Education Research Institute (TERI) in Matsumoto, Japan. There she studied with Dr Suzuki himself.

Lois was a member of the Sydney Symphony Orchestra and taught in several New South Wales and Victorian schools. For many years, she was an examiner for the Australian Music Examinations Board. She has been a lecturer at the State College of Victoria Institute of Early Childhood Development and taught violin and viola at the Conservatorium of Music in the University of Melbourne. For a time, she was Professor of Viola and Director of the Suzuki Program at Western Illinois University in the United States.

She has taught and researched the Suzuki Method since the early 1960s.

Despite the fact that she didn't set out to produce professional musicians, a very great percentage of Lois's students have become professional symphony or chamber music players or Suzuki violin teachers. Former students have won scholarships to tertiary institutions such as Melbourne University, New England Conservatory in Boston, The Juilliard School of New York, Southern Illinois University, the University of Michigan and the Royal College of Music in London. Dozens of her students won music scholarships to private schools in Melbourne.

Lois continues to give instruction to both children and teachers in Melbourne.

Her musical career ran parallel to her family life. Her son is now the IT Service Delivery Manager for Australia at a leading international engineering and construction company. Her daughter also undertook the training course with Dr Suzuki and teaches the violin and violin pedagogy in Germany. Lois has two grandsons, both students, in Australia.

**Glass House Books**
an imprint of IP (Interactive Publications Pty Ltd)
Treetop Studio • 9 Kuhler Court
Carindale, Queensland, Australia 4152
sales@ipoz.biz
ipoz.biz/GHB/GHB.htm

First published by IP in 2012
© Lois Shepheard, 2012

All rights reserved. Without limiting the rights under copyright reserved above, no part of this publication may be reproduced, stored in or introduced into a retrieval system, or transmitted, in any form or by any means (electronic, mechanical, photocopying, recording or otherwise), without the prior written permission of the copyright owner and the publisher of this book.

Printed in 12 pt Book Antiqua on 14 pt Copperplate Gothic Bold.

National Library of Australia
Cataloguing-in-Publication entry:

Title:   Memories of Dr Shinichi Suzuki : son of his environment / Lois Shepheard.

ISBN: 9781922120137 (pbk)

Subjects:   Suzuki, Shin'ichi, 1898-1998.
            Violinists--Japan--Biography.
            Music--Study and teaching (Early childhood)

Dewey Number:   787.2092

## Contents

| | |
|---|---|
| About the Author | i |
| Prelude | 1 |
| Development | 3 |
| History and Environment | 6 |
| The Suzuki Method Comes to the West | 14 |
| Memories | 18 |
| Waltraud Suzuki | 54 |
| The Son of His Environment | 61 |
| Life in Matsumoto | 66 |
| Cherished Memories | 72 |
| At the Kaikan | 74 |
| Nurtured by Love | 99 |
| Later Years | 100 |
| Finale | 108 |
| Coda | 114 |

*Memories of Dr Shinichi Suzuki*

*When the human race created the culture of speech and writing, it also produced the sublime culture called music. It is a language that goes beyond speech and letters – a living art that is almost mystical.*

*Man is the son of his environment.*

*Every child grows in the same way as he is brought up.*

*Every child can be educated.*

*Parents who have smiling faces have children with smiling faces.*

– Shinichi Suzuki

# 1
## PRELUDE

Dr Shinichi Suzuki insisted that the learning of music is similar to the acquisition of speech. He said that a child who can speak his mother tongue can be taught anything.

With the passing of time his Suzuki Method[1], now taught worldwide, is changing and developing. That is what Dr Suzuki envisaged. But as modern children and teachers, who never met the master, create their own picture of Shinichi Suzuki, he is becoming just a name, just the word 'Suzuki', or a characterless cardboard cut-out, or a God-like figure.

He would have laughed at this last image.

In Japan Dr Suzuki was the recipient of the Third Order of the Sacred Treasure, Gold Rays with Neck Ribbon in 1970. The Emperor named him a Living National Treasure.

He was awarded several honorary university degrees in the US, including doctorates from the University of Rochester at Eastman, Oberlin College and the Cleveland Institute of Music. He received the Spectrum Award of the World Organization for Human Potential in 1973 and was named String Teacher of the Year by the American String Teachers' Association in 1964.

In Europe he received the prestigious Ysaye Medal (Belgium, 1969), the Palmes Académiques

---

[1] See *Coda* for a brief explanation of practicalities of the Suzuki Method.

(France 1982) and Des Bundesverdienkreuz 1 Klasse (Germany, 1985).

Other awards included the Albert Einstein International Academy Foundation Medal for Peace, 1990 and the Rotary Service Award (Rotary International, 1960 – 61).

In 1993, Dr Suzuki was nominated for the Nobel Peace Prize.

He remained humble despite all this acclaim.

I was fortunate to be in Japan when few older foreigners were there and to be able to spend a good deal of time with him. I'd like to try to sketch his likeness for you. What I recall most is his single-minded determination to impart his knowledge of the sound of the violin, his constant statement that every child can be educated, his honesty, his unfailing sense of humour and always his complete and utter humility.

My verbal pictures of the great man are as they occurred to me; events are not necessarily in chronological order. I have added for your interest some additional recollections of my visits to Japan, maybe a glimpse into Dr Suzuki's environment.

This book also contains some reminiscences by Australian teachers who spent a long time studying with Dr Suzuki when I was in Japan. They are Marjorie Hystek, Anne Lewis and Lesley Priest.

The short quotes from Dr Suzuki (always in italics) were either spoken or written in his texts:

*Nurtured by Love.*

*Ability Development from Age Zero.*

*Ability is Not Inborn*

– Lois Shepheard, June 2012

# 2
## DEVELOPMENT

*Man is the son of his environment.*

*Man is born with the laws of heredity and develops with the laws of ability.*

Dr Suzuki insisted that musical talent isn't present at birth and that what *is* inborn is a <u>power</u>, leading to the <u>ability to adapt to the environment</u>. There is also an <u>inborn desire to change</u>.

He wrote that the inborn power:

*silently prepares for functional changes and adaptations*

and that:

*Differences in hereditary quality exist in the sensitivity and speed of the response.*

*Ability is not inborn.*

*People are born with hereditary physiological differences, but I believe that a person's abilities grow and develop depending on stimulation from the outside.*

*Education is the way to develop ability.*

*Even though people go so far as to talk of 'a born artist', they do not mention 'a born green grocer'.*

*No child is born with the musical scale.*

Shinichi Suzuki was the son of his environment.

There was hardly a musician in Europe who believed talent isn't inherited.

In Venice in the early eighteenth century, there were four church schools where orphans and illegitimate children were brought up at the State's expense and trained to be musicians. At one of these institutions the red headed priest and violinist, Vivaldi,[2] taught little girls to play instruments and formed them into an orchestra. A 1739 document states that this group ranked: 'first, for the perfection of its symphonies' and that it played with 'well-drilled execution'. The writer went on to state that the young string players had more 'attack' (from the bow stroke) than the orchestra of the Paris Opera.[3]

Despite the success of this experiment, European musicians stubbornly and arrogantly refused to believe that musical talent was anything but innate. The concept that every child could be educated, even to music, really had to occur to someone taking a fresh look at education; someone with no background at all in Western musical tradition with all its preconceived ideas. This someone was in Japan. Shinichi Suzuki came to the realisation that, with the right training, anyone could play music well.

> *As long as the spectre, ability-and-the-inborn, hovered in the air, educational circles would remain haunted; bewildered by the inborn gift and ability, educators would be unable to comprehend the essence of the development of human ability.*
>
> Society at large was convinced that children who are poor at such subjects as maths ... have poor brains... I realised however, that these children ... speak Japanese with

---

[2] Antonio Vivaldi c.1675 – 1741.

[3] *Dictionary of Music and Musicians* (Grove).

*absolute fluency and moreover, freely utilise a vocabulary committed to memory with as many as 2,000 words at age six…*

*They had wonderful brains! Depending upon how they were raised, children beautifully demonstrated their ability.*

In explaining the cultivation of ability in little children, Dr Suzuki used many analogies. One was the story of a seed planted in the ground. We can't see the development of the plant as the sun shines on the earth and the rain nurtures the seed, but one day a flower appears. Similarly, he said, we can't see the development of a child's ability but must keep nurturing until the flower unfolds. It is an example of the universal law of cause and effect. As the Bible says, 'As you sow, so shall you reap'.

All history is the result of countless successions of planting, nurturing or not nurturing. The history of the Suzuki Method is no exception.

So, you ask, why did this particular seed need to be planted and cultivated in Japan? How did it produce such a splendid flower?

I remember that, years ago at a Buddhist centre in Melbourne, I told a priest about Dr Suzuki and his work. The priest said, 'There are those who choose when and where to be born.'

Perhaps he was right… and Shinichi Suzuki was born not only for today. He is timeless.

# 3

## HISTORY AND ENVIRONMENT

Japan was almost entirely isolated from the outside world from the early 1600s when foreigners, particularly Christians, were forced to leave the country. Foreign contact ceased and ports didn't reopen to trade for some two and a half centuries.

Suzuki was born in a country that had been, as he wrote, 'denied cultural history that belonged to the West'.[4] In the same book he writes of Western musical instrumental history:

> ... *beginning with an instrument with a wound string, manufactured in antiquity and found in a pyramid in Egypt... and that history proceeding through time, till the birth of what sings of man's soul and is called a violin.*

He was born on the seventeenth of October 1898, the third son of the seven boys of Masakichi Suzuki and Ryo Fujie. Shinichi also had five sisters. His parents were from prominent samurai families. His mother had attended a singing school and played the shamisen.[5]

Samurai served the landowner-warlords (*shōgun*) and samurai levels were hereditary, ranging from the upper samurai to the lower foot soldiers. This structure was Japan's system of government.

---

[4] *A Philosophy of Performance – 30 Years' Meditation on Sound* (Shinichi Suzuki).

[5] A three-stringed, banjo-like instrument.

*History and Environment*

In 1853 a US naval fleet of two sailing boats and two steamers, under the command of Commodore Perry, sailed into Tokyo harbour. Perry had been ordered to facilitate trade and diplomatic contact with Japan. He went to Tokyo again in 1854, and a treaty of friendship was signed.

When the Japanese people became aware of Western achievement and systems of government, there was tremendous unrest. Just seventeen years later, the Japanese, with their great propensity to institute change, abolished the system of warlords and samurai. The country was thereafter governed by a centralised system of Western type bureaucracy and very soon, a prime minister and cabinet.

So in 1871, Shinichi Suzuki's grandfather was out of work and the twelve-year-old boy, Masakichi (who was to be Dr Suzuki's father), was no longer destined to be a samurai. In 1873 Masakichi began working for his father, a manufacturer of shamisen. Then he became an English teacher; he'd attended an English school for two years as a youngster. He also learned lacquer work and began training as an elementary school music teacher.

In 1877 when Masakichi turned eighteen and, as was the custom, became head of the family and financially responsible for it, he started making shamisen. In 1884 a violin was taken as a curio to Japan. Masakichi borrowed it, made some drawings and measurements and in 1888, after many experiments, successfully produced the very first Japanese-made violin. At first he sold his instruments to the Nihon Gakki Co., then in 1900 he opened his own violin factory in Nagoya. This establishment also manufactured mandolins and guitars. By 1910 it was producing 65,800 violins per year. By 1930

Masakichi Suzuki had established three factories in Nagoya and employed about 1,000 workmen.[6]

As they grew up, Shinichi and his brothers and sisters played on the factory floor, marching pieces of violin around like dolls. Violins were a natural part of their childhood. Masakichi sent Shinichi to commercial school so he could later assist with the violin business. When he graduated, Shinichi started in the factory office, in charge of export. One night, full of curiosity, he took a violin home, together with a recording of Elman[7] playing Schubert's *Ave Maria,* and started to teach himself to play. He was seventeen. He began to consider actually making violins himself saying at the time: 'In order to produce a good violin, I thought it necessary to play the violin.'[8]

He developed some sort of lung problem and his father sent him to Shizuoka Prefecture to recuperate. There he met the Prince Tokugawa. At the suggestion of this affluent Prince, Shinichi went to Tokyo to learn the violin.

Remarkably for that time in Japan, his Tokyo teacher was a woman, Ko Ando.[9] She first studied with the Austrian music educator, Rudolf Dietrich[10] who had been imported by the Tokyo Music School. After her graduation in Tokyo, Ko Ando went to Berlin (1900) as a student of the great teacher, Joachim.[11]

Apparently, Joachim was one of those who

---

[6] *Universal Dictionary of Violin and Bow Makers* (Henley).

[7] Mischa Elman, eminent Russian violinist (1891 – 1967).

[8] *Suzuki Changed My Life* (Masaaki Honda).

[9] Ko Ando (1878 – 1963).

[10] Rudolf Dietrich (1867 – 1919).

[11] Joseph Joachim, Austrio-Hungarian violinist (1831 – 1907).

*History and Environment*

influenced his students by example, performing during lessons to keep their enthusiasm. It is said that he was unable to give a verbal explanation of violin techniques.[12] We do not know what type of tuition Ko Ando gave Suzuki.

Again the Prince Tokugawa stepped in, recommending that young Shinichi should continue his studies in Germany. Shinichi knew his father would be strongly opposed to the idea. The Prince suggested some subterfuge was necessary and laid out a plan. Shinichi told his father that he'd like to accompany Prince Tokugawa on a world tour. Masakichi was pleased with this arrangement, gave his son ¥10,000, and said farewell. The "world trip" ended in Germany. Shinichi Suzuki was 22.

Ko Ando was aware of the ruse and had offered to give the young violinist introductory letters to some of the important violin masters in Germany but Suzuki preferred to observe teachers for himself and make his own decision.

He chose to learn from Karl Klingler[13] (another former Joachim student) after hearing a performance by the Klingler Quartet. The few performances of this quartet now available on CD[14] indicate that Klingler was indeed a fine musician and a fine player. About 1890, however, Flesch[15] wrote of Klingler: 'he has not yet succeeded in getting away from the spiritual fetters of his teacher which have held him in bond for 30 years.'[16] As we listen to the quartet today, we can presume that Klingler was a thinker, probably

---

[12] *Memoirs* (Carl Flesch).
[13] Karl Klingler, German violinist (1879 – 1971).
[14] Recorded 1905-1936. The CD now on 'Testament' label.
[15] Carl Flesch, Hungarian violinist (1873 – 1944).
[16] *Memoirs* (Carl Flesch).

keen to experiment, and that he broke free of those fetters.

The young Suzuki was told that Klingler never took private pupils. However, he approached the violinist and asked if he could possibly audition. No doubt Klingler would have been intrigued to see what a young Japanese student had done with the study of the violin. Suzuki played a *Concerto* by Rode and clearly played it well; Klingler chose to teach him. Suzuki stayed for eight years, spending four years studying sonatas and concerti and four years on chamber music, Klingler's area of expertise.

A particular Berlin professor became Shinichi's friend and something of a protector. On one occasion when this professor was going to be away from Berlin for a period of time, he asked another good friend to keep an eye on the naïve young Japanese man. The man was Dr Albert Einstein. Einstein played both the violin and piano.

Germany made a tremendous impact on Shinichi Suzuki. Apart from anything else, of course, he couldn't speak German as well as the little German children.

'I did have great difficulty with the language,' he said. 'I could not understand what people said nor could I express my desires in words. I did not think that I was a dunce – I had been a bright student in school – but with German, I was like a retarded child.'[17]

He was introduced to the evening concerts held in the homes of Berliners. This type of entertainment had become very popular; it gave the German people a chance to escape from the disorder of a country still settling down after WWI.

[17] *Suzuki Changed My Life* (Masaaki Honda).

*History and Environment*

At one of these soirées he met the violinist Albert Prange and his sisters, a singer and a pianist. Shinichi fell head over heels in love with the singer, for her sake converted to Catholicism, and married Waltraud Johanne Prange in 1928. Waltraud was seven years his junior. The wedding was an elegant affair; the couple travelled in a black wedding coach, driven by coachmen in top hats and walked into the church on a long red carpet.

Suzuki had completed his studies, when he and Waltraud decided to go to Switzerland to live. His mother became ill, however, and he had to return home. His new wife was very lonely in Japan. She told[18] how uncomfortable she was with the admiration she received if she ventured out (these were days when foreigners were rarely seen in Japan) and took to just wandering round the garden instead.

Shinichi's father, Masakichi, fell on hard times and Shinichi sold his beautiful Vuillaume[19] violin to help him out. When Masakichi asked Waltraud to sell her valuable piano, newly arrived from Germany, she agreed. She also agreed with her husband that they shouldn't return to Europe.

Shinichi formed a quartet with his brothers who had been studying with Ko Ando. A string quartet was a rarity in Japan and not particularly understood by the general public – apparently not by radio announcers either. Shinichi's viola playing brother, used to become quite carried away during performances and sometimes nearly stood up. The quartet's first radio broadcast therefore became a disaster when the violist left his chair and the announcer thought

[18] *My Life With Suzuki* (Waltraud Suzuki).
[19] Jean Baptiste Vuillaume, French violin maker (1798 – 1875).

he wanted it taken away. Decades later, when Dr Suzuki related this story, he still laughed heartily at the incident.

On one occasion, his quartet was rehearsing and Shinichi's nieces and nephews were playing nearby, chattering away happily. He thought how well the German children had spoken German, how well Japanese children spoke Japanese and…

He stopped playing and cried out, 'All Japanese children speak Japanese.'

He chuckled when he told us of his brothers' reaction. They weren't at all impressed by the interruption.

We can imagine their comments: 'Oh, get on with it now brother, of course they do. What else would they speak? We have a concert next week. Please pick up your violin and play!'

But Shinichi Suzuki had realised that if children could learn their mother tongue, they needn't fail to learn anything. He thought how children brought up in Tokyo spoke with a Tokyo accent and if they came from Osaka, the accent was completely different. He asked himself how this was possible and how could children assimilate such subtlety?

> *I learned that the natural method of teaching a child its mother tongue is a marvellous educational process. It is a natural process in which practice continues from morning till night.*
>
> *Every child in a nurturing environment grows steadily and without mishap toward involvement in the activity of speech and responds according to the stimuli supplied by the parents.*

It was obvious to Suzuki that if parents played recorded music to their children every day, those children would easily learn to understand the language of music. An appropriate teaching method and the parents' assistance at home could train youngsters to reproduce that language.

Can you imagine the excitement of that young man? There he was at the very dawn of a new culture in Japan and he was dreaming up a new concept. It would be like an early Australian settler coming to a new way of life; it would be like discovering the Internet!

Suzuki began to devise his teaching method in the 1940s. On August 15, 1945, the Emperor of Japan, understood to be a direct descendant of the Sun Goddess, spoke on the radio to his people for the very first time. The shock of this broadcast must have been quite considerable. The Japanese people had neither heard his voice nor been allowed to look on his face. In this "Jewel Voice Broadcast", the Emperor announced that the conflict was terminated, saying the 'war situation has developed not necessarily to Japan's advantage' and that the nation must 'bear the unbearable and endure the unendurable.'

He spoke to a population whose polished and disciplined lifestyle had been reduced to a state of the most terrible ruin. There was a tremendous need to lift the spirits of the defeated, depressed Japanese people and Shinichi Suzuki felt his method of music education might be one means of accomplishing this.

# 4

# THE SUZUKI METHOD COMES TO THE WEST

*Every human ability is a talent.*

About 1960, footage of little Japanese violinists was shown on Australian TV. We watched a Japanese phenomenon, scores of little children all playing well and directed by a man called Suzuki. Their performance was reported to be the result of this man's new method of music teaching. I was intrigued, obtained a set of the violin instruction books from Japan and began experimenting with my own pupils.

The violin books came with little coloured, see-through plastic records – performances of groups of violinists, not of Dr Suzuki's playing. This helped lead to the mistaken idea in the West that the method's lessons were done in classes.

In 1967 I went to live in New York with my husband and our two children. There I visited schools that taught what they called the "Suzuki Method". America had been short of good string players for the major symphony orchestras and had set up string classes in the elementary schools. When education authorities saw Suzuki's Japanese Mother Tongue Method of Talent Education they attached the name "Suzuki" to their already existing class tuition and

## The Suzuki Method Comes to the West

America had the Suzuki Method.[20]

Of course these were early days in the history of the Suzuki Method in America and the teachers I unwittingly watched were amongst those who adopted the word Suzuki without the method. There have always been excellent Suzuki teachers in the United States and today there is a multitude of fine Suzuki teachers and students.

The New York classes I observed had mixtures of violin, viola, cello and maybe double bass pupils, say 30 per class, beginning at the age of about ten. There was no parental involvement, though Dr Suzuki stipulated that parents should play a huge part in assisting with the study process. Nor did there appear to be a recording to listen to – no musical "mother tongue". This despite the fact that the class music books were *Listen and Play* by Professor John Kendall[21] based, with Dr Suzuki's permission, on Book 1 of Suzuki's Violin School. (The original Suzuki Book 1, and therefore *Listen and Play*, contained the first nine pieces of the modern *Suzuki Violin School Book 1*.)

Many of those early teachers had entirely missed Suzuki's principle that music heard daily can be learned as easily as a language heard daily and that therefore the children should be listening to recordings. In addition, the American classes gave rise to the mistaken belief that Suzuki students learned in big groups rather than by individual instruction.

---

[20] At the time, Dr Suzuki was not comfortable with the word "Method". His wife always maintained that the use of that word introduced an element of inflexibility in people's thinking about her husband's teaching.

[21] John Kendall (1917 – 2011) leader in the early days of the Suzuki Method in the United States.

The New York teachers I watched, eager to teach a good playing technique managed after a year to get children to play the rhythmic *Twinkle, Twinkle Little Star Variations* and *Lightly Row*. That's just the first two pieces in the book. I could see the Suzuki Method wasn't working wonders for them!

When Dr Suzuki came to New York for a seminar, I attended this and had some private sessions with this master. At the time, he made little impact on me. I perceived he was earnest and had charisma but I'd seen the Suzuki Method taught very badly and judged that it didn't work in the Western world... I couldn't yet speak Japanese and Dr Suzuki's English was very poor. (It was always weak. He could easily mix Japanese, English and German in one sentence.)

> *Every child can be educated but please don't educate like my English; my English made in Japan.*

I took my very young daughter, Cathy, to have a lesson from the great man. She was like many a little one – she refused to play. (Cathy now teaches the violin and violin pedagogy in Germany at the Robert Schumann Hochschule in Düsseldorf and the University of Cologne.)

I was bewildered when Dr Suzuki told me his students started to learn to read music at the age of seven, once they could play the Vivaldi *Concerto in A Minor* and I came to the conclusion that since young New York children couldn't play at that level, then Japanese children must be very different from Western children. I saw Suzuki several times working with the Americans. The way he taught bore little relation to what I'd seen in New York schoolrooms.

## The Suzuki Method Comes to the West

I thought I should go to Japan and watch Japanese teachers and Japanese children. When I did go (that first time with Sydney teacher, Harold Brissenden)[22] I made arrangements to visit child-minding centres, primary schools, high schools, universities – and guess what? I found that Japanese children are just the same as any others!

---

[22] Pioneer of the Suzuki Method in Australia.

# 5

# MEMORIES

I'll never forget the first time I heard a group of Japanese children playing in real life. Despite all the TV coverage I'd seen, I was quite unprepared for the impact this performance would make on me. I was near tears as I watched a large group of students aged no more than nine playing Bach's *Concerto for Two Violins*. As I remember the event even now, I have a lump in my throat.

I attended some Suzuki Method Teachers' Conventions in Honolulu. I remember at one of these, sitting at dinner with a very international group. As far as I can recall, it included Professor William and Constance Starr[23] from the US, Dr Honda[24] from Japan and Dr Alfred Garson[25] from Canada. We were entertained during dinner by a group of little Japanese violinists. It hit me suddenly what a heavy responsibility we have, guiding children. The group on stage trusted their teachers implicitly and had been taught to play beautiful music.

'You could train a group of children, anywhere in the world, to do anything,' I mused as I listened

---

[23] William Starr, violin teacher and Constance Starr, piano teacher, pioneers of the Suzuki Method in the United States.

[24] Masaaki Honda, leader and supporter of the Suzuki movement in Japan. Dr Honda led the overseas concert tour groups of Japanese Suzuki children.

[25] Alfred (Henrik) Garson, one of the first exponents of the Suzuki Method in Canada.

to Mozart. It was a very sobering and somewhat disturbing thought.

Looking at my old programmes, I notice that one of the young soloists at a Honolulu conference was a lad by the name of Haruo Goto. Haruo now teaches in Sydney.

Dr Garson told us about one of Suzuki's early visits to Canada. Alfred had set up a lecture/demonstration. The visiting Japanese children performed a most difficult programme and then the audience was invited to ask Dr Suzuki some questions.

A nun rose and proceeded to explain her difficulties with teaching.

'Professor Suzuki, I have a number of students,' she said. 'They don't have good posture and I just can't get them to hold the bow correctly. They never seem to be able to play a piece from memory; they just don't have the confidence. They don't play well in tune either. What should I do?'

Suzuki's answer was immediate.

'Pray to God,' he said (as Alfred Garson reported).

## GOING TO JAPAN

As soon as the Western music world became aware that hundreds of Japanese children played the violin, foreign teachers began to visit Dr Suzuki's studio. He welcomed them all and was generous with his information. I was one of those who began to make repeated trips to Japan.

Suzuki's home was in the city of Matsumoto in Japan's Nagano Prefecture. It lies between the Japanese Alps and the plateau of Utsgushigahara.

The first time I got off the train at Matsumoto, I was confronted with a country town. Facing the station, the shops and restaurants had the traditional navy-blue curtains over the doorways so you had to bow your head to enter. A couple of visits later and I found the railway station had a paved taxi rank area with a uniformed taxi official in charge, a department store across the road and a "Kentucky Fried" in the main street, complete with a large Colonel Sanders on the footpath. It was sad in a way.

A few years after that, someone put a hole through that Colonel Sanders' head…

Suzuki taught in the *Kaikan* building of Talent Education,[26] just along the road from the NHK[27] building. There used to be a park in front of the Kaikan. I took some Melbourne teachers and my daughter there for a few weeks. Cathy had turned fourteen and I wanted her to again meet this man with his very special mind. I wouldn't have worried at all if she'd had no lessons from him. However, we went when it was the New Year holiday and there were temporarily no teacher trainees or children in the Kaikan. To demonstrate his teaching, Dr Suzuki took advantage of Cathy's presence and gave her at least one lesson every day. What an opportunity for her (and me!)

By this time, Dr Suzuki was elderly and his vibrato had become very slow. (Vibrato is the fast wavering of pitch, done by the player's left hand. It looks as if the violinist is shaking the hand/arm.) I asked him one day how he taught it.

'I say, "Don't play like Suzuki",' he replied.

Later on, when I got to know him well, I would never have asked such an impolite question.

---

[26] Opened in 1967.

[27] Japan Broadcasting Company.

*Memories*

Dr Suzuki with Lois's daughter, Cathy, aged 14.
Note the picture of Kreisler on the wall.

His early recordings of the pieces in his violin books show a very well controlled vibrato, as do recordings from the string quartet he had with his brothers. Likewise a performance of the César Franck *Sonata* (Berlin c. 1928) shows him well in control of vibrato speed as a young man.[28]

In the earlier years of his teaching, Suzuki concentrated on left hand techniques but later his focus was on the right arm. We remember he studied with Karl Klingler who, Flesch said, 'divulged the secrets of the bow arm'.[29]

(Here again we have evidence of Klingler's ability to change. Just twenty years before that statement, Flesch wrote that Klingler: 'possessed

[28] Issued on CD by Symposium Records: *The Great Violinists Vol. VII.*

[29] *The Art of Violin Playing* (Carl Flesch, 1924).

great technical and musical talent, which however did not fully mature, owing to the peculiarities and shortcomings of his training. His bowing technique was dominated by the fallacious theory of the lowered upper arm and the "loose" wrist.')[30]

Instructing his teacher trainees, Dr Suzuki corrected the right arm but merely commented on any left hand techniques such as intonation[31] or vibrato; he didn't offer instruction in these areas. I never heard him mention any other aspects of left hand or arm technique.

## THE SEARCH FOR SOUND

Suzuki's trust in his mission, to listen to and teach the sound of the violin, was absolute. It was, he said, the reason for his existence.

His awakening to "sound" occurred when he heard recordings of the violinist, Fritz Kreisler[32] and the cellist, Pablo Casals.[33]

> *30 years ago, my ears first heard the splendid sound of Kreisler and Casals; it was sound coming from recordings but it was to me, as that joyful sound, full of life, rang out, exactly as if my Zen master had said, "Teacher, sound is to be your kōan".*[34]
>
> *Since then, I have meditated before that magnificent sound, listened at all times to the sound, thought to follow that sound and to solve the kōan has become the reason for my existence...*

---

[30] *Memoirs* (Carl Flesch).

[31] Pitch control.

[32] Fritz Kreisler, Austrian violinist (1875 – 1962).

[33] Pablo Casals, Spanish 'cellist (1876 – 1973).

[34] *Kōan* = riddle.

*With this truth before me, I was a lone traveller on a journey in the search for sound... My efforts have extended the boundaries of my mental capacity.*

*I hear the two masters' tone. I think it is their words to which I devotedly listen. It's as if the two of them surpass all wise men. Kreisler's sound, Casals' sound, both have taught us natural, rational truth...*

*In response to the Zen kōan, I obtained the absurdly simple and unquestionably Eastern answer:*

*"It is the natural form of the strings as they reverberate."*

*This humble answer illuminated for me a new path of performance practice pedagogy.*[35]

A follower of Zen Buddhism strives to achieve the flash of *satori*, enlightenment/<u>intuition</u>, by meditating on a *kōan*.

As a man of Zen wrote: 'intuition is a function which we all possess but which very few of us can use at will.' ... 'It is the inspiration of the artist, poet, the highest awareness of the greatest scientist and thinking musician.'[36]

D.T. Suzuki wrote: 'When a man's mind is matured for *satori* it tumbles over one everywhere ... a blooming flower or a trivial incident.' He likens the flash of satori as similar to: '... the light touch of an igniting wire, and an explosion follows which will shake the very foundation of the earth.'[37]

---

[35] *A Philosophy of Performance – 30 Years' Meditation on Sound*. (Shinichi Suzuki).
[36] *Teach Yourself Zen* (Christmas Humphreys).
[37] *An Introduction to Zen Buddhism* (D.T. Suzuki).

And from Dr Shinichi Suzuki:

*The vital power of intuition must be developed until it becomes a power that is unrestricted.*

*Without training, intuition (just like other abilities) cannot grow.*

At the Kaikan we had our lessons on tone production, always on tone.

*Please play to Kreisler.*

*So deep, so deep a tone.*

*So light a tone, two horse-hair only.*

*Beautiful tone, beautiful heart.*

*Tone has a living soul. It breathes, without form.*

Sometimes Suzuki would ask, 'Who is your teacher?' That meant, 'To which violinist's recording are you listening?'

*After the lesson I ask, "who is your teacher?" And the student answers, "Kreisler". Then I laugh and say, "Give my regards to Kreisler".*

Students often had to play to the photograph of Kreisler which hung on the studio wall.

While the young Shinichi Suzuki was in Germany, absorbing European culture and the music of Fritz Kreisler, other violinists were also noting Kreisler's tone quality. In 1924, Carl Flesch wrote: 'Fritz Kreisler ... has arranged for himself a technique of tone-production ... He uses but little of the bow, strong pressure[38] and a continuous, most intensive vibrato ... achieves the highest measure of expression

---

[38] Translated into English as 'pressure'. I would prefer to say 'weight'.

... what results might not a Method bring about, which raised Kreisler's purely personal means of expression to a generally current law?'[39]

In the same book Flesch writes: 'One should be careful not to regard too many things as gifts of nature. Colour and volume of tone, bowing and finger technique, an ear for proper intonation – all these may be acquired and improved, because the functions of the organs which participate in them are susceptible to verification, and are accessible to external influences. On the other hand, a man's nature and mode of feeling are given qualities, and can only be altered when his inner consciousness, as a consequence of one or another influence, undergoes a change...'

Flesch couldn't have guessed, in Berlin in 1924, that the "method" he pictured would be devised by a young man studying in that same city, but with his roots in the Orient. Suzuki was certainly alerted to "sound" in Germany; on his return to his home country, he married those European concepts with what was purely Japanese.

I was lucky in that my main teacher at the NSW State Conservatorium of Music had come down the same violin technique line as Dr Suzuki's German teacher. We all owed our violin lineage to Joachim. When I saw Suzuki's bow technique, I soon recognised it.

Suzuki's ability to determine the cause of any tonal deficiency, as far as bow technique was concerned, was impressive. I was a professional player before I went to him and he certainly could still alert me to tonal shortcomings. Though, when an old man, he couldn't necessarily demonstrate a

---

[39] *The Art of Violin Playing* (Carl Flesch).

required change of technique, he'd quietly say, 'I cannot do, but I can say something.'

## THE RESEARCH STUDENTS

Those who went to Dr Suzuki for long-term training were called *kenkyūsei* (research student). The course was officially of three years' duration but it was up to Suzuki to decide how long a kenkyūsei stayed there. We were allowed to graduate only if he were satisfied we would know how to analyse our pupils' playing and develop a range of techniques appropriate to various styles of music.

> *In considering "technique ability", technique is perhaps best viewed as a broad category of "expressive or performance ability".*
>
> *Technique is not just proficiency of hand movement, but the ability to phrase beautifully with good intonation and expressive tempo.*

He always discussed arm/hand/finger movements in terms of the muscle movement, arm weight, finger weight, thumb pressure etc. as necessary for a particular sound. He used purely physical terms rather than any imaginative metaphors. Of course he was teaching adults and his kenkyūsei would need to eventually convert the wording to something understandable by children.

He insisted that the bow shouldn't be held too tightly, preventing necessary changes of finger/thumb weight. Students holding too firmly were admonished with:

'No! You have bow in hand!'

*Never push.*

Each private lesson we had with our master was very short, perhaps twenty minutes. Firstly there was the tone quality exercise with suggestions for improvement and a little practice, then a technical exercise of some sort, everyone being set the same one over the course of a week. This was very often the one that had emerged as his latest "new idea".

*I have new idea!*

The exercise was corrected and practised; then we played the piece of music we'd been preparing, Suzuki decided on a point for improvement and suggested a technical exercise. He didn't explain to which particular section of the piece it related. The kenkyūsei's task was to think it through, work out where the change was required and incorporate it into the next lesson's performance.

Suzuki advocated the "one point lesson", i.e. we were advised never to swamp our pupils with too much information nor confuse them by asking for too many corrections to be made. The art of the skilful teacher is to note the imperfections and find the one correction which will also pull other techniques into line. In fact Dr Suzuki offered many "points" in the course of a lesson but they all aimed at the same ultimate improvement.

Cathy returned to Matsumoto as a kenkyūsei. After she'd been there for twelve months, Dr Suzuki told me she could graduate immediately but she and I decided she should stay another year.

One of her Japanese friends had already spent seven years studying to be a violin teacher; I noted she was still there many years later. There were some who weren't allowed to graduate.

Kenkyūsei lessons were recorded. Though they were short lessons, there were occasions, as I listened to my tapes, back in my apartment, when I thought, 'I forgot he said that.'

That in itself is a lesson! With the best will in the world, a student doesn't always take in and remember all that happens in a lesson. Probably with our pupils we can expect about 70% retention of information.

The kenkyūsei called me *Kiyashi no okaasan* (Cathy's mother) and addressed me simply as *Okaasan* (mother). This was always my name, even after Cathy graduated and left Japan. I was everybody's okaasan and many a kenkyūsei came to tell me of his woes. The other kenkyūsei, of course, were all about Cathy's age.

Dr Suzuki considered that a German kenkyūsei's violin wasn't nearly good enough for her needs. One day he decided to do something about it.

'Have this one,' he said to her.

The violin he gave away was one his brother had made – very precious…

An American kenkyūsei who had no money turned up for a lesson with only three strings on his violin. Suzuki gave him the wherewithal to pay for a new set. Eventually, when this lad needed to return to the US, Suzuki bought the lad's instrument for a ridiculously high price, enabling the purchase of an airfare.

Our master had a little cache of ten yen coins which he had built up by fining kenkyūsei if they played the "first finger" out of tune. That's the index finger of the left hand and notorious among string players as being the one to slip a millimetre or so along the string, ruining the intonation. The little box filled very quickly and then it was time to throw a party. There was always a prize for the kenkyūsei least fined! (When we were there, the exchange rate was 400 yen to the Australian dollar so a ten yen piece was equal to two and a half cents.)

One foreign kenkyūsei played quite badly. He had been admitted to the training course but somehow, despite all Dr Suzuki's instruction, made no progress. He was always placed last on the (weekly) Monday concert programme so that everyone, except Dr Suzuki, could leave the hall before he began to play. He never graduated.

## THE SPIRIT OF REPETITION

We were encouraged to practise everything:

> *10,000 times only.*
>
> *Knowledge plus ten thousand times is skill.*

A foreign kenkyūsei took Dr Suzuki at his word and tried to practise everything 10,000 times. She kept tally, documenting every piece and exercise by number and date in an exercise book. We all hoped the girl wasn't setting herself up for a good bout of Repetitive Strain Injury!

After that particular kenkyūsei left, someone found her book and gave it to Dr Suzuki. He was highly amused and showed it to everyone enthusiastically. Shinichi Suzuki was certainly an exponent of the Zen truth: "If you lose the spirit of repetition, your practice will become quite difficult."[40]

---

[40] *Zen Mind, Beginner's Mind* (Shunryu Suzuki).

Dr Suzuki's spirit of repetition often needed to come to the fore when he taught foreigners. If the kenkyūsei didn't understand the instruction in either Japanese or in Suzuki's English, it was quietly and patiently repeated.

Teaching little children Dr Suzuki often used what he called "Matsumoto Mathematics"; this was a new system of counting for teachers.

'Can you play it five times correctly?'

The child sets off as the teacher counts.

'One, two, two, two, three, three, three, three, three…'

Before he first decided which pieces of music to include in the violin instruction books, Suzuki experimented with some traditional Japanese songs. There is one about a sparrow learning to sing at the school for sparrows. (*Chi chi pa pa chi pa pa…*)

'I had student, I teach this song every day, every day six months,' he said. 'The student ask if he can learn new song. So I write new song. Every day, every day six months I teach new song.'

The new song was *Allegro* in Book 1 of the Violin School and not so very different from *Chi chi pa pa*.

Beside the now familiar violin books, Dr Suzuki produced many texts,[41] most of which are not available today. They include:

From the 1930s: *Practising Kayser Studies* (Heinrich Ernst Kayser's studies for young violinists).

1940s: *Violin Practice and Performance*

*Quint Etudes* (For training good intonation).

---

[41] From *An Examination of the Suzuki Method* (Fumiyo Kuramochi).

**1950s:** *Research and Reflection on Performance Practice and Pedagogy*

*Note Reading on the Violin*

*Songs Transcribed for Ensemble Pieces*

*Japanese Pieces for the Violin*

*Encore Pieces for Playing at Home*

*Home Concerts Vols 1 & 2*

**1960s:** *A Philosophy of Performance, 30 Years' Meditation on Sound*

*A Guide to Tone*

*Researching Kreisler's Performance*

*An Instructional Method for the Violin*

Suzuki told me he was going to remove the *Sonata in F* by Handel from Violin Book 6, and replace it with something else. He said his books contained 'too much Handel'.

*I have new idea!*

He told us about the time he worked in the violin factory. The first time he mentioned it to me, he was speaking English and it was quite a while before I realised the "fabric" was *fabrik* – the German word for "factory".

When he was in junior high school he got a summer job at the factory, rising at five to start work at seven. His working day finished at five in the evening. He said this routine contributed to his self discipline and he thought it would be excellent if all kenkyūsei could spend some time in similar employment.

'But,' he said, smiling, 'No one will try it!'

His energy was truly amazing. On one occasion, he went to Denmark for a seminar. I was going with him but there would have been problems with my Japanese visa.

(I'd bought a Danish phrase book though, and it was helpful, having on the cover: *Dansk – Japansk*. That stopped the would-be English students on the train. I generally had to give impromptu English lessons on the way to and from Tokyo and this I quite enjoyed doing, but if I needed to work at something else, I held this little book in front of me and it was a great deterrent.)

Coming back from Denmark, Suzuki flew from Copenhagen to Tokyo, took the bus from Haneda airport to the city, made the four hour train ride to Matsumoto, was driven to the Kaikan, climbed two flights of stairs to the main hall, strode straight to the front of the kenkyūsei class and literally jumped up to stand on a chair and teach. He was already in his 80s.

He'd told all the violin kenkyūsei to learn the little Dvorak *Sonatine* while he was away. In this first class after his return, he decided we should all play it with a recorded accompaniment. He chose a kenkyūsei to conduct us and was highly amused when our conductor couldn't bring us in together on the first note.

Now, a conductor controls the start and tempo of a piece. When he raises the baton ready to begin, he does so at the precise tempo he wishes the piece to go. That up beat indicates to the players exactly how to proceed. They begin to play when the baton then drops to its lowest point, ready to bounce up again. The conductor can't give the timed up and down beat if someone else is putting a recording on somewhere, controlling the opening of the music so he doesn't have a clue when it will happen. For all of us to start at the right split second was nigh impossible.

Suzuki laughed at us, wishing we'd learn to be quicker off the mark. A musician needs to learn to think at speed. For instance, if a string quartet is performing and the second violinist changes the interpretation slightly, the other musicians have just a *split second* to hear, notice, process the information, make a decision and send a message to their muscles to play some matching sound.

When he was over 80, Suzuki could still challenge a young kenkyūsei to a race and win it; three times up and down his quite long studio.

### 'Must Have Been Nice'

He had the greatest sense of humour. He and I we were upstairs in the Kaikan hall, listening to a teachers' orchestra rehearsing on stage. It wasn't good; there was much stopping and starting. Dr Suzuki pulled on his cigarette (chain smoker, 50-60 per day, Camel cigarettes, unfiltered), put his head back and listened.

Suddenly, he sat forward and called to the stage, 'What are you playing?

'Mozart,' was the reply.

He nodded a few times and took another puff of his cigarette before he turned to me.

'Was Mozart,' he said. 'Must have been nice.'

> *It was Mozart who taught me to know perfect love, truth, goodness and beauty.*

> *Children in their simplicity seek what is true, what is good, what is beautiful, based on love. That, I believe, is "the true nature of man" as described by Gautama Buddha. Mozart, whose music taught me the simple love and joy that overcomes misery, must have believed that too.*

We remember that Dr Suzuki's definitive book on his philosophy is called *Nurtured by Love*.

I went with him to Nagoya to a cello concert. There was only one violin item, a group of very young children tearing through Fiocco's *Allegro* at maximum speed.

'Japanese speed,' said Suzuki.
'Yes,' I answered.
'Easy piece,' he muttered.
'Yes,' I said.
The violinists were already well into their performance, they were going so fast.
Suzuki nodded a few times admiringly then turned to me.
'Easy piece,' he laughed. 'But not for teachers…'

*Easy piece.*

Even if playing at "Japanese speed", one has to observe the rests in a piece of music – the moments, sometimes only split seconds, of silence. Dr Suzuki called them "very important nothings".

He insisted he was an amateur. It was one of his jokes. He meant it in the true sense of the French word *amateur*, "one who loves". Some foreigners misunderstood and took him at his word but I can't think of anyone more professional.

He loved music.

> *Music is the language of the heart without words.*

He told us of the time he was teaching the bow exercise we all know as "panda", as yet unnamed. The big graduation concert[42] was coming up in Tokyo and he thought it should have some publicity. So an article was sent to the *Mainichi Shimbun* and he looked forward to seeing it in print.

On the day, about three centimetres of newsprint in one of the paper's columns detailed the concert. The rest of the newspaper was filled with an article and pictures of the new zoo panda just acquired from China.

'So,' said Suzuki. 'If we want publicity we must mention "panda". From now, this bow exercise is called "panda".'

To this day, many foreign teachers think "panda" is a Japanese technical term and many Japanese think it has something to do with a technical term in English...

The Kreisler Highway is another one of his jokes. That's where the violin bow should travel over the strings, close to where they cross the violin "bridge". Suzuki understood this was the best place for sound production, and was where Fritz Kreisler must have run his bow. Since there was a car manufacturer called Chrysler, Suzuki named the spot the Kreisler Highway. It wasn't such a leap of imagination in Japanese. In that language "Kreisler" and "Chrysler" are written the same way.

---

[42] Children work through a series of graduation levels. The certificates have a painting by Dr Suzuki of the Japan Alps surrounding Matsumoto.

After WWII, goods marked "Made in Japan" were considered substandard. Dr Suzuki took advantage of that concept:

> *Every child can be educated but please don't educate like my English; my English made in Japan.*

There was a class up in the Matsumoto Kaikan hall every Friday when teachers from the surrounding area came in. I joined it every week too. One day, Suzuki had us do knee-bends as we played, to discourage any body tension. There was a visiting American teacher in the class.

'It's like Japanese toilet training,' the American said. (Japanese toilets are level with the floor. You have to squat to use them.)

Dr Suzuki heard the remark and thought it was terribly funny. He called it the "toilet training exercise" for a long time afterwards.

As he listened to Monday concert items (or indeed to some performances in his teaching studio), Suzuki often appeared to fall asleep but was immediately alert when the kenkyūsei stopped playing.

I asked him once how he kept going through his long hours of teaching.

'Oh,' he said. 'When a student plays, I decide in the first two minutes what I'm going to teach and then I sleep till he finishes.'

### 'I'M BECOMING SEVEN'

He met me early at the Kaikan one morning saying: 'Come now. Come and see.'

He had a video of two violin students practising

at home. The elder girl was eight or nine and played Kreisler's *Praeludium und Allegro*. Its level of difficulty is comparable with at least Book 10 of the Suzuki Violin School.

Then it was the two-year-old sister's turn. She was learning to play the first *Twinkle* rhythm on her E string. No way. The mother tried everything. The dolls were lined up to listen to the concert; the child was encouraged to practise so she'd be great for the teacher next lesson or able to play for daddy when he came home.

Bribery with sweets.

Nothing doing.

The little one wanted to play *Praeludium und Allegro*. So the sisters played it together. The two year old played everything on the note E. Every stroke of that 1/32 size bow was in time, in the right direction, using the same bow speed, identical with that of her big sister. She had watched that piece being practised for hours on end and had thoroughly absorbed it.

Suzuki was known to say it should take six months for a beginner violinist to learn the first piece in Book 1, *Twinkle, Twinkle, Little Star Variations*, and then a further six months to finish the book. I guess he said it to guide some teachers who were hurrying students off the *Twinkle* variations before their techniques were sufficiently stable and that the statement was then proclaimed as "Suzuki law". It certainly caused me the occasional headache as a Melbourne parent came across it and thought his or her child wasn't doing well enough. Dr Suzuki was the first to confirm that there were no hard and fast rules as to a child's progress.

Advancement on a musical instrument depends on so many factors: the child's age, his physical co-ordination, the amount of music heard in the home, the number of times a Suzuki recording is played per day, the amount of time spent practising, the general attitude of the parent etc.

In Melbourne I had a student who went through Book 1 in three months, another took five years. One student took three years to learn *Twinkle, Twinkle* and went on to study music at university; another took two years to make her way through Book 1 and in a further two years had finished Book 7, at the age of nine. Note that there are pieces in Violin Book 6 upwards, which are also prescribed for the Victorian Certificate of Education examination (at a student's final year of school).

I was at the back of a near empty hall, watching a leading teacher, Miss Mori, take a group class on stage when Dr Suzuki beckoned to me from a front seat. I dutifully made my way forward to see what interested him.

He was laughing at a child in the second row of violinists. The little soul was playing some Vivaldi but was so tired, she was nodding off. Her arms and fingers kept going as she swayed back and forth, side to side. Then she'd wake with a start, as one does from an illicit nap, and jerk herself into a more energetic performance. The children around her looked at each other, giggling, and paid more attention to their sleepy friend than to Miss Mori or Vivaldi. Of course the inevitable happened and the little girl fell forward into the front row.

From about 1970 Suzuki didn't teach children consistently, It was generally Miss Mori who provided the opportunity for lesson observation. She taught in the nearby *Sumisu* (Smith) building and is the finest of teachers, an expert with youngsters.

The gentle Mrs Toba was also an excellent person to watch. She handled her pupils with kindness and tact and clearly understood Dr Suzuki's philosophy of "nurturing by love".

In Japan, it is bad manners to blow one's nose in public; it's more appropriate to sniff. If you have a terrible cold, you should wear a mask. I observed a youngster one day, having a lesson from Miss Mori, on the second movement of the *Concerto* by Mendelssohn. Her mother had a terrible cold and stood behind the girl, carefully following the music score.

Mendelssohn's beautiful slow movement was punctuated by painfully loud sniffs.

I watched Mrs Kataoka's piano lessons; she taught at the Kaikan and together with Mrs Suzuki of Tokyo (Dr Suzuki's sister in law), devised the Suzuki piano course.

Kenkyūsei were required to attend classes in interpretation held by Mr Takahashi, who established the Suzuki Flute School. This teacher stressed the importance of relating instrumental music to what would be sung, in terms of musical line, phrasing and appropriate tone quality. The class heard recordings of instrumentalists and singers, Takahashi's favourite singer being the tenor, John McCormack.[43]

At first Dr Suzuki hadn't been keen on a Suzuki flute method. He always insisted that his method was based on the sound of the vibrating string. He soon accepted that, as the stream of air vibrated through the flute, the principle was the same and the cover of the first editions, called *Takahashi Flute School* had "Suzuki Method" in smaller letters at the top right.

---

[43] John Francis Count McCormack, Irish tenor (1884 – 1945).

Dr Suzuki was about to enter a room to take a class of quite young children. He stopped outside and I looked at him enquiringly.

'I'm just getting ready. I'm becoming seven,' he said and we went in.

He used to say he prepared himself for a child's mind by remembering down to the little one's physical limitations and up to his sense of wonder.

There were many Japanese violin students aged less than two. If there were to be a children's group class in the Kaikan hall, everyone had to make their way up a couple of flights of stairs. If the chubby little legs were too short to climb the steps, the mothers carried children and violins up; those babies performed their Handel and Bach and were carried down again.

Little children playing in the sandpit listened to their music through headphones, a tiny tape player strapped to their backs.

On one occasion Suzuki came, slippers and cigarette, along the corridor.

'Come listen,' he said.

I went into his private studio. He had a tape of a seven year old girl playing the *Sicilienne* by Paradies. It was beautiful playing.

'It must only be a quarter size violin,' I said. "What a beautiful sound! It must be easier on a quarter size violin!"'

Suzuki looked at me doubtfully. I thought to myself: "Silly me! If I joke in English, he won't understand."

The next morning he was waiting for me at the front door, beaming, with: 'I have new idea! Now we all play quarter size violin...'

*I have new idea!*

That occurred when he was hearing children's graduation tapes and that particular year there were nearly 8,000. He started listening to those tapes at 5am every morning. As I sat and noted the care and patience with which he considered every performance and recorded his comments, I marvelled again at his tirelessness.

There were many very young Japanese violin students – perhaps seven or eight year olds – finishing Book 10. Once when Suzuki had just returned from America he said as he indicated levels with his hands: 'It used to be Japanese children abilities so high, American so low. But now, American children also so high.'

Then he laughed proudly, saying, 'But Japanese children so high, so young.'

## GOD-LIKE?

One evening, Dr Suzuki took a group of young foreign kenkyūsei to a French restaurant in Matsumoto. After the meal, the 83 years young Dr Suzuki set off along the street at a very brisk pace. The nervous foreign students followed him at a discreet distance to see that he was all right. Then they realised that this person, whom they deemed quite superior (god-like?), was really like everyone else and could get about in the real world outside the doors of the Kaikan quite satisfactorily.

He told us he'd decided, decades before, never to get angry. Once I saw him irritated when teaching the Martini *Gavotte* to a group of youngsters. He took the wrong turn in the piece, left the stage and didn't come back. His mind must have wandered to something else.

In that piece the theme returns repeatedly, followed each time by a different tune. I always impress on my little students they must get the route sorted in their heads and then concentrate, otherwise Martini's *Gavotte* could continue going round and round and last for about three days…

There was a time Suzuki was irritated with me. His "new idea" was to put the right hand thumb down into the curve of the frog (at the end of the bow, where the player holds it), way below where the thumb normally sits. I hadn't done that, because I'd just come from Tokyo with a beautiful, brand new, gold mounted, tortoise shell frog bow and the corner of that new frog was quite sharp. If I shoved my thumb down into the "u" shaped bit, it would hurt.

Dr Suzuki grabbed my thumb and jammed it down.

It hurt.

He told us how, as a young man, he'd gone up into the mountains and learned how to be a healer. I watched him heal people on several occasions. It appeared to sap a lot of his energy. I've seen children who'd fallen and hurt an arm go happily back into a class after a few minutes of his ministrations.

'Now you go play,' he'd say.

I saw an American boy with a fairly severe leg injury of several months' duration, limp toward Dr Suzuki and 30 minutes later, walk away easily.

Some Zen training is described as channelling the healing vibrations available in nature.

Lesley Priest remembers the moment when Dr Suzuki first laid his hand on her shoulder to help her upper arm relax as she played. She said: 'I had developed a habit of tightening and raising my right shoulder when pushing the bow upward. In that first nervous lesson with the master in Matsumoto, the tension in my shoulder was even greater. It was Suzuki's touch that brought real awareness to my mind and body. It was a touch that I felt tingle throughout my whole being and that enriched my soul.'

Suzuki told us he'd learned to withstand cold and heat and that, as part of his training, he'd grasped white hot metal. He never wore a coat, even in the depths of Matsumoto winter.

It was suggested to me recently that stories such as the above may have contributed to Westerners' God-figure image of Shinichi Suzuki. For all his declarations that he was a Catholic, Suzuki was a son of Japan and of his era. We note the writings of D.T. Suzuki: 'I make bold to say that in Zen are found systemized, or rather crystallized, all the philosophy, religion, and life itself of the Far-Eastern people, especially of the Japanese.'[44]

Certainly, those who study Zen can develop, among other attributes, indifference to the discomforts of heat and cold.

Suzuki said that when he was young, he used to pray at the Shintō shrine and that his father instructed him to give thanks for what he had; never to ask for anything extra.

Since about 1600, Japanese people have followed both Shintōism and Buddhism. Christianity was re-introduced about 1853.[45] In 1871, freedom of religion was decreed. Today, Japanese people celebrate life's main events – birth, marriage and death – by the rites of different religions.

---

[44] *An Introduction to Zen Buddhism* (D.T. Suzuki).
[45] Francis Xavier had previously introduced Christianity in 1549 but it was banned in the early 1600s.

However, many aspects of Suzuki's character are reminiscent of pure Zen practice: his uncomplicated, open ways, his lightness of touch, his lack of pride. Apart from his study of Zen texts, he had a Zen master, his great uncle, Fuzan Asano, head priest of Chusenji Temple.[46]

A Zen master said: 'Without any intentional, fancy way of adjusting yourself, to express yourself as you are is the most important thing.' And again: 'If your practice is good, you may (might) become proud of it. What you do is good, but something more is added to it. Pride is extra. … Get rid of the something extra.'[47]

Dr Suzuki's lack of pride was always apparent, whether he were dealing with adults or children. One morning when I arrived at the Kaikan, I found him in the foyer, playing a game with a young boy. The lad had brought his "Simon" game, a plastic box with four big buttons each of which played a note when pressed. The box played a random selection of notes and the player had to press the appropriate buttons to copy it. Suzuki looked at me and laughed; he was choosing to play the wrong responses. The boy was thrilled – he was "beating" Dr Suzuki!

## TONE HAS A LIVING SOUL

Sometimes a kenkyūsei might play badly in a lesson with Dr Suzuki. As he or she finished the piece, there'd be a nod of our master's head, the cigarette would be placed carefully on the ash tray, then Suzuki would pull himself resolutely from his

---

[46] *Shinichi Suzuki: The Man and His Philosophy* (Evelyn Hermann).

[47] *Zen Mind, Beginner's Mind* (Shunryu Suzuki)

comfortable chair in the corner and walk, nodding and laughing toward the player.

'So miserable!' he'd say.

He pronounced "miserable" with the accent on the "a"; it sounded rather French. He followed the word with the reminder:

> *Tone has a living soul.*

He was always full of energy. One would find that elderly man on the floor, up on a chair, exchanging bows and violins with students, bending his body backwards, dancing around a class. Underneath this hilarity he was the perfectionist, aiming for the finest violin tone.

Without a good sound, a violin is just another tool.

## 'IF YOU THINK OF DOING SOMETHING, DO IT'

One of the teachers told Dr Suzuki that a much older child wanted to start learning the violin.

'Then quick, start!' returned Suzuki urgently. 'Before he gets any older!'

A particular adult was having lessons from Dr Suzuki. For months the man struggled, not very successfully, to master fingering and bowing techniques. Suzuki was more interested in helping this man reach a goal than have him become a successful violinist.

> *To surrender to the thought of having no talent and give up the effort is cowardly.*
>
> *To lament lack of ability is folly.*
>
> *Every human ability is a talent.*
>
> *If you think of doing something, do it.*
>
> *Please try...*

There was a very pregnant foreign kenkyūsei. Dr Suzuki laughed and patted her affectionately on the shoulder when he was faced with the dilemma of her protruding belly getting in the way of her bow stroke.

## Respect

Dr Suzuki related how during the war, the violin factory in Kiso Fukushima prepared wood for the manufacture of float planes. Suzuki, as plant manager, took over a wooden clog factory and used its timber. He found the way to good productivity was to treat his workers as family – as equals.

This is of course how he treated everyone, be they parents, teachers, kenkyūsei or indeed students of any age. It is why I mentioned at the beginning of this book that he would laugh to think he was considered a sort of God-figure…

*I respect all living things.*

He used to say we should talk to people we met in public such as passengers on a train. They were placed there by destiny.

'They know something you don't know,' he said. 'You'll probably learn something.'

Shinichi Suzuki had an extraordinary ability to engage and communicate with an audience. I went to a lecture given to townspeople in the Matsumoto City Hall. As I walked out I heard several people say, 'He was looking at me all the time.'

He was always outspoken when lecturing to parents. He wondered if sometimes their commands at home were:

'Do your practice!'

> *There are those who think that this constant nagging is education. This method can be called the "How Not to Develop Ability" method.*
>
> *Parents who have smiling faces have children with smiling faces.*
>
> *The child's face shows his parents' history.*
>
> *Every child grows in the same way as he is brought up.*
>
> *Anyone can be raised to be musically tone deaf.*[48]

Our master was a deep, analytic thinker. His lectures to teachers, parents and the general public were always delivered in the same quietly confident fashion. He had a sense of humour and a lightness of touch but his message was direct and serious.

He could get carried away and speak for a very long time. If his wife were on stage with him, she'd tug at his coat to let him know he'd said enough.

There was the time he was giving a lecture to violin teachers who all listened with rapt attention. Suddenly, to everyone's consternation, his trousers began to slip down. (He disliked belts and braces.) Not noticing, he kept going with his energetic lecture, gesticulating and walking up and down the stage. The stripe of white underpants, showing above his trouser waistband, grew larger and larger.

'Why doesn't he notice that?' I asked myself but I knew why. He was too busy delivering his message.

---

[48] Unable to discern musical pitch.

Mr Hirose, a leading teacher from Tokyo, came down the aisle from the back of the hall. He bowed politely, left and right, smiling in embarrassment at the audience which was by now not paying any attention whatsoever to Dr Suzuki's lecture. We were mesmerised by the underpants. Reaching the stage, Hirose attracted Suzuki's attention. Suzuki leant down and the teacher whispered in his ear.

Dr Suzuki looked at his trousers.

He stood up and pulled at his waistband as he jumped high into the air.

'Now I have good tone,' he cried triumphantly.

At the end of the session he was besieged by dozens of teachers offering good advice and safety pins.

## INDIFFERENCE TO MONEY, FAME, POWER

Dr Suzuki was the most straightforward person one could meet; he was so impeccably honest himself, that he trusted everyone. He had no concept whatsoever of duplicity. He would sign anything if asked, without reading or understanding the document. If someone asked for a signature, then they wanted it and he could give it. There have been many teachers who went out into the world with a paper signed by Shinichi Suzuki, giving them permission to do whatever.

For all he wrote in some texts about principle and interest, he really had no concept of money or business methods.

As R.H. Blyth writes: 'A deep love of poetry, of nature, of music will make a man correspondingly indifferent to money, fame, power.'[49]

Suzuki used to announce with much laughter,

---

[49] *Zen and Zen Classics Vol 1.* (R.H. Blyth).

'Time is money.'

He had the power to laugh at all things, beginning with himself.

His wife wrote: '... my husband was and never has been concerned with money.'[50]

In the same book she wrote of their early impecunious days of marriage; 'unlike my own experience through World War I, for him money had always been there. He always took taxis.'

She goes on to say that her husband could use the last of their cash for a taxi fare and when chastised, laugh and go to borrow from one of his brothers.

## THE WHITE HOUSE

Suzuki Method tour-groups of ten outstanding young performers gave concerts overseas. Dr Suzuki told me laughingly of an occurrence in Washington. One of the children, Sayō-chan, was asked to perform at the White House with eleven year old Amy Carter. Amy was a Suzuki student and the daughter of the US president. I first heard Sayō-chan when she was four, giving a marvellous rendition of Dvorak's *Humoresque*. At the time of her invitation to the White House, Sayō was an advanced player.

She was told she would play two pieces with Amy. Not knowing which of the many pieces in the ten Suzuki books and additional repertoire these would be, the little girl practised all day and missed the sightseeing excursion with the other Japanese children. She duly went to the White House and found it was to be the first two pieces in Book 1.

Suzuki gave me a copy of his address to President Carter, written in March 1978. The preliminary

---

[50] *My Life With Suzuki* (Waltraud Suzuki).

remarks lay the groundwork for a plea for the establishment of A National Policy for Nurturing Children from 0 Years Old. In part it says:

> *Mr President, and Members of the Senate and House of Representatives, we appreciate from the bottom of our hearts this opportunity of your devoting attention towards world peace and the welfare of all people.*
>
> *I think that it is a miserable and sad thing that various countries have armed forces and continue to increase the strength of their armaments. Constantly somewhere on the earth there are countries fighting each other and killing people. This is our history from ancient times. Many fine people have devoted themselves and made great efforts to bring peace to the world, but in spite of that, the world is not changed. It remains in a miserable condition, as it used to be.*
>
> *WHY?*
>
> *The basic reason is that almost all of the children in the world are not given any education at the crucial age of zero years old. We can shape the destiny of the children to become people with beautiful hearts, or wild people like beasts; but very few people know this fact...*
>
> *The common sense of the world gives us the wrong belief that 'our hearts and ability are inherited'. This wrong concept is still believed today, but it is the greatest mistake of humanity...*
>
> *I noticed that every child in the world has the potential to be developed very highly in faculties other than their mother tongue. It depends only on the method of education. The*

> secret is in the "mother tongue method." This is really a very clear thing that has been proven right in front of our faces. EVERY <u>child in the world can be educated successfully, IF we use the right method</u>...
>
> Every child's heart and other abilities can be shaped according to the method of rearing and nurturing. The method of nurturing from the age of zero decides whether the baby is superior or inferior, beautiful or ugly, virtuous or viceful. I learned that children can be destined in <u>any</u> way...
>
> ... Once, about twenty years ago, I shed tears in the middle of the night thinking of all the babies born on the earth which were in a miserable state because they were being educated in the wrong way.

The education plan is then outlined. The home of every newborn baby should be visited by an advisor and the parents given guidance as to how to educate the child, how to keep him in good health and how to raise him to be "a fine human being". This specialist visitor would continue to watch the child's progress for some five years. If the family were too poor to educate their child, they should be given government assistance.

Members of Congress no doubt listened with varying degrees of comprehension. In some, there might even have been a trace of wistfulness. All would immediately have considered the tremendous cost of such a project and a few may have got as far as weighing it in their minds against the necessary spending cost of national defence. Dr Suzuki, honest, earnest and sincere, no doubt hoped he had planted some seeds of compassion in terrain owned by the great master, Dollar. Of course Suzuki was right; in a

Utopian world, his proposal would work.

As each different reader reads this book, he understands differently. Each member of an audience hears and comprehends a musical performance differently. President Carter and his members of Congress all heard the words Dr Suzuki uttered and listened with varying degrees of sympathy. The fact remains though, that any group of politicians, at any time and in any country, would place more value on defence spending that on the education of the country's 0-year-olds.

For all Dr Suzuki's earnestness, his message was to be applauded and forgotten.

## Outto!

Our master insisted that the whole body is involved while playing the violin, just as it is when playing a sport. He'd demonstrate the action of a baseball pitcher. He did a marvellous imitation – with a chuckle at the end.

Commentary for baseball matches on TV was (naturally) in Japanese till the commentator slipped into English: 'Strikie one! Strikie two! Strikie suree! 'OUTTO!'

Suzuki might call out, 'Strike' when a little violinist child achieved accuracy in a musical passage.

In Matsumoto, in the middle of his teaching, our master would leave his studio and we'd all wait till he returned from watching a sumo contest on TV. He loved watching those huge men wrestling. I was amused at that. They were such a contrast to his small frame.

*Memories*

He insisted that a violinist's stomach should be firm, and asked me to punch him while he played. You know, despite his urging, I really couldn't punch Dr Shinichi Suzuki in the stomach.

# 6

# WALTRAUD SUZUKI

I remember Waltraud Suzuki so very well, her big bosomed, deep throated voice (remember she was a singer), her jaw quivering with her loud laugh, her thick German accent.

What an extraordinary woman she was! To marry a young Japanese and go to live in Japan in 1929 when there was hardly a foreigner to be seen in that country, would have taken a lot of courage.

In the first instance, she handled all foreign mail. She was as able in English as she was in German and quickly became fluent in Japanese. It was no mean feat for a German lady to translate *Nurtured by Love* from Japanese to English. After that particular task, she said she wouldn't care if she never saw another Chinese character again!

The Japanese language is written in three different scripts, all mixed together. The Chinese "letters" (*Kanji*) are those complicated characters imported from China in about the fifth century. A little First Grade child learns 46 of these as well as the hundred or so phonetic letters of the other two scripts. Then the number of Kanji is increased yearly till he knows 1,850 by the time he leaves school.

One needs considerably more than 1,850 to translate something like *Nurtured by Love*. A kanji dictionary is not arranged alphabetically and, I can assure you, is a great trial for a foreigner to handle.

Sometimes it was found necessary to change or

simplify the writing of certain kanji. These would be shown on TV. Waltraud Suzuki used to get so cross about this.

'How stupid!'

It was tricky enough for us foreigners to commit hundreds of kanji to memory, without finding them altered.

Suzuki's mind was only on his teaching. He would discuss tone quality any time, at the dining table, on the stairs; even in the gentlemen's toilet if he met a kenkyūsei there.

> *Education means to teach and develop.*
> *Without development there is nothing.*
>
> *Every child can be educated.*

His ever caring, devoted wife understood Shinichi Suzuki's simplicity as well as his brilliance. Since there was no room in his thinking for the ordinary things of life, Waltraud dealt with all those.

'Ach, that man, Suzuki!' she laughed, fondly. 'Every morning he asks where is the orange juice. And every morning I say the orange juice is in the refrigerator where always is the orange juice. Ach! That man!'

> *If there is no one to take care of my meals, I don't eat a bit all day long; but fortunately my wife sees to it that I have proper nutrition.*

One freezing winter's day she and I were talking when Dr Suzuki approached us, all excited because he'd noticed everyone in the street wearing head phones. He concluded that the people of Matsumoto had decided to listen to music.

His wife dashed his eagerness with, 'They're ear muffs, not head phones. It's cold, Suzuki!'

As he shuffled off she again laughed her jaw-shaking laugh.

'Ach, Suzuki! That man!'

Waltraud lived all her married life in a cigarette smoke filled home (the 50-60 Camel cigarettes per day).

'Ach, that man,' she said. 'He kills me with his cigarettes.'

Mrs Suzuki eventually died of emphysema in 2000.

Dr Suzuki told us that when he was young he saw a picture of the world's oldest man. It was a Russian with a cigarette in his hand, so Suzuki determined that to attain a long life he too must smoke. It must have worked; he passed away in his 100$^{th}$ year.

He was given a beautiful new violin case but wouldn't use it because he could fit more packets of cigarettes in the old one.

He said he practised smoking, ready for the time he would be a better teacher and would have time to smoke.

Marjorie Hystek remarked that though she adored Dr Suzuki, she dreaded her lesson time in his studio when the winter was cold, snow and ice fell from the rooves of nearby buildings and all the Kaikan windows were closed.

'Suzuki's room was shrouded in cigarette smoke,' she said. 'How he lived as long as he did is still a mystery but I was fortunate in that he was there for me.'

I squirm inwardly, feeling real shame when I remember that I often gave Dr Suzuki gifts of Camel cigarettes.

Mrs Suzuki still came to watch her husband teach.

Even after decades of marriage, she was still interested. One day she and I were sitting together when she suddenly said in a low voice, behind her hand: 'That is not his violin. Where is his violin?'

'I don't know,' I said quietly.

I looked hard at the instrument Dr Suzuki was playing.

'You're right,' I whispered.

Eventually Mrs Suzuki could bear it no longer.

'Where is your violin?' she demanded very loudly.

'It's gone to the repairer,' Suzuki answered nervously.

'That's all right then,' barked his wife.

It seems there might have been a history of misplaced instruments. When my daughter was a kenkyūsei, Dr Suzuki lent her his Stradivarius[51] violin. Well, I'm not sure whether it really was a genuine Strad but it had a beautiful sound. Two years later, the day before she left, she returned it.

When she came back to Matsumoto about twelve months later, Dr Suzuki was clearly pleased to see her.

'Where is my violin?' he asked.

My daughter Cathy was *really* perturbed.

'I gave it back,' she said. 'You told me to put it on the shelf in your room.'

It was a mystery! The violin was not to be found. Then Suzuki remembered he'd lent it to a missionary fellow, an amateur violinist, some months before, and forgotten about it entirely.

---

[51] Antonio Stradivari (1644-1737), universally known as the greatest violin maker.

Life continued to be difficult for Waltraud Suzuki, even after all those years in Japan. I was with her at a hotel desk in Tokyo when she asked for the key to her room and the desk clerk, looking alarmed, made a phone call:

'There's a foreigner asking for the key to Dr Suzuki's room,' he said, thinking that she and I wouldn't understand what he was saying and entirely forgetting he'd just been asked in Japanese for that key.

Mrs Suzuki strode off, exasperated.

'So stupid!'

I told the desk clerk who she was. He was suitably abashed.

I have confronted panic when I approached a desk clerk or shop assistant or waiter etc. Once when I went to buy tickets for a *kabuki* (classical drama) performance in Tokyo, the man behind the counter ran off and returned many minutes later, very flustered.

'There isn't anyone here who speaks English,' he said in Japanese.

'But I asked in Japanese for tickets,' I replied in Japanese.

Or the restaurant waiter who panicked when I sat at a table.

'We don't have any bread,' he stammered.

He was comforted to find I ate rice. I just *had* to tell him we grew rice in Australia and exported it to Hong Kong...

Mrs Suzuki and I went to hear the results of an American kenkyūsei's English teaching. His little students were going to perform a play about Humpty Dumpty. We sat with the parents and waited for the

*Waltraud Suzuki*

Dr and Waltraud Suzuki (right) with Lois.

drama.

Unfortunately no one had been well enough drilled and all each actor could remember was: 'Oh! What a big egg!'

Mrs Suzuki was peeved. When she told her husband, he shook his head, disappointed.

Being married to a singer, Dr Suzuki naturally became aware of vocal practice techniques, including "Vocalization" exercises. For a singer, this is the exercise and control of the vibration of the vocal cords, to open up the voice. Suzuki coined the word "Tonalization", the exercise of control over the vibration of the violin string. Over the years in which I had contact with him, he always began lessons with his Tonalization exercise printed at the beginning of Violin Book 2.

Once when I was back in Australia, Mrs Suzuki rang me from Matsumoto.

I'd done an interview with a newspaper reporter and his article appeared in the British *Telegraph*. He'd asked me about my earliest contact with Suzuki students and I told him that when I first saw the method in New York, I made the mistake of thinking it wouldn't work with Western children.

The reporter put his own slant on my words and wrote that I'd 'dismissed it as brainless rubbish'. Someone in England sent Mrs Suzuki a copy of the paper. She was hostile! I told her not to believe everything she read in the newspapers.

Perhaps this is where we remember the writing of a Zen scholar: 'bull-fighting is bad, and newspapers worse.'[52]

---

[52] *Zen and Zen Classics Vol. 1*. (R.H. Blyth)

# 7

## THE SON OF HIS ENVIRONMENT

Many a tired kenkyūsei heard Suzuki's same kind words: 'Here, take this 10,000 yen. Go and buy a steak.'

I don't think Dr Suzuki ate much steak. He told me he practically lived on nattō (fermented soybeans). The sticky nattō is apparently good for the health but it's so evil smelling I couldn't come at it at all.

He hated the notion that patience was needed when teaching.

*You don't say, "I'm patiently eating a steak".*

One thing he didn't eat was the traditional New Year rice cake (*omochi*). It's so glutinous that every year many elderly Japanese choke to death on it. Suzuki laughed at the ridiculousness of that.

'So stupid!' his wife growled.

He may have laughed at the problem of the rice cake but Suzuki was still the son of his environment.

One day he told me he intended to give a recital when he turned 80.

'What will you play?' I asked him.

'Oh, Brahms, Beethoven.'

He paused.

His wife said: 'Brahms! Beethoven! Ach! And you know what he plays? Taka-taka-ta-ta,' (That's the first rhythmic variation on *Twinkle, Twinkle*).

From the eighth century, the custom of celebrating old age, beginning with the 40th birthday, was adopted from China and some of the special birthdays are still celebrated in Japan.

On the 80th (*sanju*), clothing, cushions, and wrapping for presents should be golden brown or yellow. I'm not sure how Dr Suzuki would have incorporated that rule at his recital...

In a music shop in Tokyo, I saw two violins made by one of Suzuki's brothers. The workmanship looked identical but one was infinitely dearer than the other. The shopman explained that the expensive one had been made when the maker was 80.

A traditional gift for 80+ birthdays is a walking stick with a pigeon carved on the handle. It's said that pigeons don't choke, so this gift is a wish for the elderly person who will probably eat a rice cake at New Year.

*Man is the son of his environment.*

I was teaching English at a Seiko factory in the evenings. I'm not much of a meat eater so when my young engineers suggested they take me out to dinner to a sashimi restaurant, I was OK with that. Silly me! I thought sashimi was always raw fish. The dictionary said "raw fish"... I was presented with a plate of raw horse meat and my English class was really cross when I just *couldn't* eat it. It had cost them a fortune.

Suzuki asked me to help the leader of the kenkyūsei orchestra, prior to a concert. We were to play one of the Bach *Brandenburg Concertos*, one with an uncomfortably difficult solo violin part. I spent some time with the young man, sorting out the necessary techniques. Though I was coaching the

*The Son of His Environment*

leader, my position in the orchestra remained the same. Foreigners were seated at the end of the sections. I was next to a nice young man whose mother was Japanese but his father was Korean. We two foreigners sat together.

Dr Suzuki asked me if I'd coach some students playing string quartets. The cellist in one of them eventually came to Australia and is Sydney's leading Suzuki cello teacher, Takao Mizushima. I seem to remember that his quartet was playing Beethoven and I resolved to have them perform at Monday concert.

On Mondays, every kenkyūsei had to perform. After each of us played, Dr Suzuki came to the stage and gave a mini lesson. The quartet I'd been coaching played well and I wondered what Suzuki would have to say.

Silly me! Why did I wonder? He told the group to move a couple of metres to the left and play again. The sound was utterly different. Dr Suzuki knew the acoustics of that hall exactly.

## This is What I Have Learned

When I first saw the Suzuki Method in Japan I was struck by its Japaneseness. I understood immediately that we Australians must adopt its educational components, not its purely Japanese content. Dr Suzuki was the son of his environment; we are the sons of ours.

Even so, I was aghast when he said suddenly, 'You don't teach Suzuki Method.'

'What have I done wrong?' I silently panicked.

'You teach Suzuki-Shepheard,' he said. 'No one teaches Suzuki Method but Suzuki.'

Of course! It could be a trap for a teacher, anxious to do the right thing by the Suzuki Method if he or she disregards what was studied and known previously or assimilated since.

Suzuki never said: 'You must do exactly as I say. I'm right and you're wrong.'

Instead his often repeated phrase was:

> *This is what I have learned.*

In the book, *The Words of the Buddha* we find the story of the blind men and the elephant. Each man was shown a different part of the elephant. One felt the leg and said the elephant looked like a pestle while the one at the tail end said an elephant was like a rope. So it is with the Suzuki Method. We all see it differently, just as we all differ in our assessment of a lecture or a performance of music or a film. It depends on how it is presented to us and on our previous knowledge and experience.

For sure, the only person ever to teach the Suzuki Method was Dr Suzuki.

Over the decades he changed many of his ideas. For instance, in the years I was in contact with him he said the practice of scales was unnecessary. His early editions of the violin books had plenty of scales. It's a mistake to think we're always following the Suzuki Method. *Which* Suzuki Method?

When we returned for a return visit to Matsumoto, Dr Suzuki would ask: 'What new ideas have you found? What have you developed?'

Those of us who have been teaching for some time, find that our teaching methods have evolved since our first experimental years. There is no recipe for teaching. As the student of Zen wrote: 'A thousand thousand men have climbed to the summit of Fuji-

## The Son of His Environment

yama in Japan to see the sun rise in the distant sea; none told the same tale of the journey.'[53]

There is definitely no formula for teaching the Suzuki Method. Sometimes an inexperienced teacher might imagine the music/instruction book itself is the "method". As the saying goes: 'a finger is needed to point to the moon, but what a calamity if one mistook the finger for the moon!'[54]

---

[53] *Teach Yourself Zen* (Christmas Humphreys).
[54] *An Introduction to Zen Buddhism* (D.T. Suzuki).

# 8

# LIFE IN MATSUMOTO

Japanese rooms are measured by how many rice straw *tatami* mats fit, each one being a little less than one by two metres. My room in the apartment house up on the Susuki River was a six mat size.

Winters are cold in Matsumoto. You have to leave the tap over the sink running at night or the pipes freeze. Sometimes they do anyway and then one has a column of ice coming down from the tap as well.

If my tap froze, it was a real performance to put it right. Put the kitchen slippers on and get the kettle from the stove; walk to the kitchen door, take off the slippers, cross the tatami in the living room; put the corridor slippers on, go along the corridor and down the stairs to the front door (dodging the sheet of ice in the hallway in front of the toilets); take the slippers off and put on the outside shoes; go into the snowy garden and fill the kettle with water from the only tap that didn't freeze. (I'm not sure why it didn't; I guess there was a hot spring there somewhere). Then proceed, reversing the slipper changes, back to the kitchen to boil the kettle and pour the water on the tap. Repeat the whole procedure till the pipes have thawed.

Some of the kenkyūsei made an enormous snowman in the park just opposite the Kaikan. It was a great snowman and I could see he just needed a violin to be complete. In the room up on the very top floor of the Kaikan there was a cheap violin lying on the floor, caseless, in the dust. I went upstairs and got it. A proper snowman now!

The next morning as I approached the snowman, I saw Dr Suzuki. He was standing, bemused, as he looked at the fragments of violin at the snowman's feet. Of course the glue had disintegrated overnight and the instrument lay in the snow in its 70 pieces.

'Who would put a violin up there?' Suzuki asked me. He was clearly shaken.

'I did,' I replied. I explained it was a cheap, Chinese[55] thing from upstairs.

'Ah, so!' he replied, unconvinced. I knew he was thinking that any violin is a violin and doesn't deserve to lie in bits in the snow…

It was Christmas in Matsumoto. The cooking facilities in my apartment were minimal but I managed to make a Christmas cake in a tiny portable, metal oven placed on one of my two gas jets. Other foreign kenkyūsei managed similar culinary marvels and we trudged through a snow storm, singing Christmas carols, to someone's apartment. There we ate our version of Christmas dinner to the accompaniment of a radio broadcast of Handel's *Hallelujah Chorus* sung in Japanese. Some choirs in Japan specialise in this piece.

There was a public bathhouse just near the Kaikan. If you remembered to take your bath things with you in the morning, you could go to the bath on the way home. If not, you had to do some extra walking through the snow.

---

[55] Chinese-made instruments for students used to cost very little and were of inferior workmanship. These days, they are well crafted and still inexpensive.

You could tell which of the naked bodies in the bath belonged to violinists. They were the ones with left hands raised in the air, out of the near boiling water, so their fingertips wouldn't get soft. The local Matsumoto ladies didn't seem to notice; they were obviously used to this eccentricity.

At first I was perturbed that the man who took the money as you entered was in full view of participants in the ladies bath. That meant we were in his full view.

'Hmmm...'

None of the other women seemed to be worried. All the same, I was much relieved the day I saw him in the street, walking with some difficulty. He was almost blind.

When I told Waltraud Suzuki I'd been concerned, but now knew the man was at least near sighted, she laughed her jaw-shaking laugh at my fears and told me about the American who'd gone to the public bath in a Matsumoto hotel (the baths take hours and hours to heat unless the water is coming directly from a hot spring) and let the water out when she'd finished bathing. As she told the story and remembered the silliness of that American visitor, Mrs Suzuki became more and more cross and I had to suggest we go out and get a cup of coffee.

We all studied calligraphy, using a brush and the block of charcoal ink. The teacher came to the Kaikan but occasionally we also had lessons at her home. In her garden a delightful little stream trickled from a bamboo pipe into a tiny pool as clear as crystal; it flowed around to return to the bamboo, beautifully elegant.

On one occasion one of the foreigners took herself outside to wash the ink from her brush…

## Life in Matsumoto

I was in an apartment house, the *Tanaka Apaato*, fronting the Susuki River. Every morning when I left the building, I turned right, beside the river, past the Coke machine with the *koi nobori* kites flying above it and on to the Kaikan. *Koi nobori* are those famous carp – the fish which bravely fight their way upstream. Isn't it a cultural contradiction to have valorous carp overlooking the cans of Coke?

Next to the apartment if I'd turned left, there was a building housing a dance school. I often heard its music.

One morning, just before I left Japan, I walked in the direction of the dance school, stood and took the trouble to read the sign outside it. There were tea ceremony classes there as well. I'd lived next to it for months and missed a great opportunity.

I went to the funeral of one of the dignitaries of Talent Education. Mrs Suzuki and the other women wore black kimono. I looked really out of place.

Most funerals are celebrated as Buddhist services. At this one, when the priest had finished with the little incense burner he came and placed it in front of me. Why he would choose an ignorant foreigner first, I can't possibly imagine.

I wafted the incense smoke towards me and now I can't remember whether I stood and let the next person kneel in front of it, or whether I handed it on. Whichever way it should have been, I did the opposite.

Wrong!

It was a huge funeral with many mourners. I was surprised when everyone was given gifts. I received several cans of beer which I gave to a young kenkyūsei.

Cathy and I went to the Shintō shrine along the river from our apartment house one snowy day, for a quiet peaceful time. Unfortunately we chose the day the priest was blessing motor vehicles. Dozens and dozens of trucks and cars were forwarding, backing and beeping, blowing out exhaust fumes and making a right mess of what had been beautiful, pristine snow.

'Oh! You shouldn't have gone *today*,' Mrs Suzuki said.

Anne Lewis longed for a conversation with someone who understood English. She bought a goldfish from the temple and talked to that. All was going well till a stray cat wandered in and ate it. Anne kept the cat, named it Pussy Chan, and remembers it was rare and famous in the neighbourhood in that it understood English as well as Japanese.

During its second winter with Anne, Pussy Chan became very ill and Anne walked the freezing streets looking for a vet. Dr Suzuki somehow heard of her plight and recommended one. When she went to settle Pussy Chan's medical bill, Anne found Dr Suzuki had already paid it.

Marjorie was sitting in the kenkyūsei orchestra when Dr Suzuki was trying to rehearse the necessary "Viennese lilt". The piano player wasn't managing it at all. Marjorie, also studying piano at the Kaikan, put her violin down and demonstrated for the girl. Dr Suzuki was very excited, relieved the poor Japanese girl of her post and made Marjorie her replacement. Marjorie was terribly embarrassed. Suzuki noticed her discomfiture and at the end of the session, went to his room, to return with a gift. It was a little alarm clock which played the Japanese national anthem as its alarm.

I was conducting the orchestra during a kenkyūsei's graduation recital. She had played the obligatory pieces from the violin teaching repertoire – the *Bourree* by Bach, *La Folia* by Corelli, the second movement of Vivaldi's *Concerto in G Minor*, then one of the big violin sonatas, the one by César Franck. We were finishing the programme with the *Concerto in A Minor* by Bach.

The student had concentrated through the long programme and played well. At the end of the second movement of the Bach, she lost concentration and played a whole bunch of wrong notes. I turned to her before we proceeded.

'Are you OK?' I whispered.

She nodded and we went on.

She and I listened to the recording of that performance many times and had a good laugh at the bizarre bit. Some months later, I chose to finish my graduation recital with the same piece. As I approached the section in question I was suddenly appalled to remember those peculiar notes. I could easily have played the same thing! It was a horribly uncomfortable sensation but it brought home to me the power of listening to a recording.

# 9

## Cherished Memories

I sometimes found Dr Suzuki playing his violin as he waited in the studio for kenkyūsei to arrive for lessons. The piece was very often *Midnight Bells* by Heuberger, something we never hear played today. He did a wonderful imitation of Kreisler's rendition: the liquid tone quality, the rubato with pulsing bow strokes especially where the composer indicates "hesitatingly".

My memory of those occasions is very clear. Suzuki would look up as I entered, move towards me still playing, look keenly into my face, then break off, take another slight step forward and lower his violin.

Then the quiet laugh.

'So I have learned.'

Back to the corner, the violin laid carefully in its case beside the chair, he sits, reaches for a cigarette, nods and eases himself back comfortably.

'So! And every child can be educated.'

He lights the cigarette, head back, eyes closed momentarily, breathes in, then sits forward a little.

He is attentive and ready for the day's teaching.

He wanted to show me how he copied the sound of a recording and chose one of Casals playing the *Berceuse* from "Jocelyn" by Godard. He played with the record, copying the tone and playing about two bars later than Casals. Then he said: 'Imitation, imitation. Yes, it is imitation but it is not so easy to imitate.'

# 10

# AT THE KAIKAN

The Kaikan has several floors. A top attic-type floor, the hall on the second, studios on the first, ground floor entrance, and below was a vault-like, smelling of tea, windowless dwelling where the cleaner *obaasan* (old woman) and her husband lived. I was never sure what the husband did, but Obaasan saw herself as running the whole establishment. She was a solid little person, perhaps 140 centimetres tall and could be so cross if Dr Suzuki dropped cigarette ash on the stairs or anywhere else. She would interrupt his lessons, bursting into the studio with a torrent of passionate criticism. Dr Suzuki always looked contrite and vowed not to be responsible for such an untidy habit ever again.

The Kaikan. Photograph courtesy of TERI, Matsumoto.

*At the Kaikan*

One of the American kenkyūsei also played the trombone and practised in the Kaikan at night. Obaasan accosted me one day with a complaint; she clearly saw me as being in charge of the foreigners. She objected to this young man making some sort of a noise in the evening.

'He goes *"bu bu bu"*,' she said.

Obaasan was most surprised when I said this noise came from a musical instrument used in Western orchestras just as a violin was.

Dr Suzuki wasn't keen on the sound of brass either. He and his wife took Cathy and an American kenkyūsei to a Rotary Family Night, as their "family". At dinner, as each course appeared, guests were entertained by a musical interlude. Suzuki enjoyed the solo from the *koto*,[56] the *shamisen*, the *shakuhachi*[57] and the *taiko* drummers who nearly deafened Cathy. Then the brass item was announced.

'Quick, quick, we go now,' said Dr Suzuki, making a determined dash for the door. His family members had to collect their belongings and hurry after him.

The kenkyūsei practice room was along the corridor from Suzuki's studio. It had a long table where each violinist sat, violin case open in front of him (for a music stand) earphones attached to a tape recorder playing an accompaniment. There is no way anyone could hear what he or she was playing or what sort of sound he or she was producing. The cacophony was considerable. If someone happened to open the windows, the neighbours complained bitterly. (You

---

[56] A 13-stringed, plucked instrument. It is Japan's national instrument.

[57] A bamboo flute.

can imagine how hot and stuffy the room was in the summer.) Dr Suzuki used to poke his head into the room and look satisfied enough with the industry. He no doubt trusted that his kenkyūsei were also practising at home and listening to the sound they produced. I generally practised in my apartment.

One day I was at the table with everyone else, surrounded by Sibelius, Chausson, Mozart, Beethoven... Someone asked me what I was practising. I had a look at the cover of my book.

'It says "Corelli",' I said.

I couldn't hear it. I was just limbering up my fingers...

It was even more difficult when I tried to play Kreisler's *Caprice Viennois* in the kenkyūsei room one day. The violinists around me were playing in the keys most used by composers of violin music. *Caprice Viennois* with its five sharps didn't fit at all. It was terribly hard to gauge what my intonation might be doing. I gave up and made myself a cup of coffee.

Visitors often gave Suzuki beautifully gift-wrapped boxes of sweets. He always brought these to be distributed in the kenkyūsei room.

Dr Suzuki decided we should play with a recorded accompaniment during lessons. His idea was that we would learn to fit in with another player and discipline our timing but some of us found the process very restricting. Cathy was preparing the César Franck *Sonata* for her graduation recital; she was already rehearsing with a fine pianist and the two had made decisions as to tempi throughout the piece. So Cathy wasn't going to play with a recording. Dr Suzuki wasn't pleased! He was thrilled

*At the Kaikan*

with her final graduation performance nonetheless. I chose generally to have lessons on the Bach *Sonatas & Partitas for Violin Solo* (no piano part…)

I saw a foreign kenkyūsei melt into tears when she couldn't fit exactly with the recorded accompaniment of the Mendelssohn *Concerto*. She was embarrassed as she left the studio and made her way toward the practice room. As soon as he could, Dr Suzuki followed her to tell her she was actually doing very well and just needed to practise another 10,000 times.

> *You don't have to practise every day; only the days you eat.*
>
> *Don't hurry, don't rest. Without stopping, without haste, carefully taking one step at a time will surely get you there.*

The Talent Education Institute kindergarten (*Yoji Gakuen*) used to be on the ground floor of the Kaikan, near the office.

In the office, Dr Suzuki's English-speaking secretary, Mitsuko, also kept an eye on the foreigners. In 2012 Mitsuko is still at the Talent Education Research Institute (TERI), helpful and sunny natured as always. Yoji Gakuen closed many years ago but the Shirayuri Suzuki Method Kindergarten, established by Mr Shigeki Tanaka under Dr. Suzuki's supervision, is still running.

I spent many, many hours watching the Yoji Gakuen class of about 60 children aged three to six and at first couldn't understand how the teacher was achieving such outstanding results. Children studied calligraphy, *haiku*,[58] maths and English conversation. They could perform the most amazing feats on miniature vaulting horses. When tested by

[58] Three line poems of five/seven/five syllables.

the Tanaka-Binet system in 1973, their average I.Q. was 158.

They could recite dozens of haiku by the poet, Issa,[59] learning 50-60 per term, and they wrote some of their own. Yoji Gakuen children would come up to me in the street to converse in English. No one else in Matsumoto could attempt to do *that*!

They were the result of Suzuki's conclusion:

> *One ability, which is sufficiently developed, breeds another, greater ability, and so on, one ability after another.*

The class started each day with a record (33rpm) of Mozart's *Symphony No. 40*, a splendid work. The children listened assiduously, all playing pretend instruments, violins, clarinets, trumpets... Unfortunately there was a scratch on the record and the needle hopped, missing a few bars. Over the years, I visited that kindergarten often and noted that in Dr Suzuki's music institute, scores of little Japanese children were digesting a slightly damaged version of a Mozart symphony. They would all have a rude awakening when they heard that symphony at a concert or on another recording. I'm ashamed I didn't mention this danger to the class teacher.

Dr Suzuki had recited haiku onto practice tapes for the children to study. Today both kindergarten children and music students study his presentation of haiku, recently issued on CD. I was pleased to get one of these as my old audio tapes had seen better days. I also have very old copies of Dr Suzuki's violin practice tapes, "Practise with me". So far, these have not been issued on CD.

---

[59] Kobayashi Issa, Japanese poet and lay Buddhist priest (1763 – 1827).

## At the Kaikan

Suzuki said how he loved Issa's haiku. He considered that the poet must have had a heart as tender as Mozart's.

'Hands clapping
Mother teaches her child
The dance.'

(Issa)

On Sundays, advanced students from around the country came to the Kaikan to have lessons from Dr Suzuki. These were generally teenagers or players in their early twenties and all performed exceptionally well. It was an expensive lesson; one paid for a month's tuition whether there for a month or just a day. So these Sunday students made it worth their while by spending the whole day watching Dr Suzuki's lessons.

One Sunday I went early to the kenkyūsei room and observed the dozen or so violinists all furiously plying their way through their concertos. Gradually they dribbled into Dr Suzuki's studio where they sat avidly taking in his comments and admiring his expertise. All except one.

As the day progressed, this particular girl didn't put in an appearance at all. She practised all day, back in the kenkyūsei room, concerto after concerto, deciding which one Suzuki should hear. As other players dipped in and out of the room to have a short practice before their own lessons or to grab a cup of tea, they noted her enormous repertoire.

Dr Suzuki wandered down the corridor occasionally too (slippers, cigarette), poked his head round the door and noted the girl practising. Bruch, Mendelssohn, Paganini… He nodded, puffed his cigarette and shuffled back to the studio.

It was time for the day's final lesson and the girl emerged from the practice room. She came in ready to impress and set about playing the Brahms.

Dr Suzuki threw himself back into his comfortable chair in the corner, took out another cigarette, lit it, changed his mind, laid it carefully on the side of the ash tray, stood up and left the room.

Brahms...

After a bit, he came back with a bag of sweets, kindly and attentively offered them to all the observers (he often did that), thought about having one himself and decided against it. He flopped back into his chair.

The Brahms player looked up a few times but continued unfalteringly.

Dr Suzuki attended to the cigarette, which by now had too much ash on it. Some dropped onto the floor and he observed it gravely. No doubt he was thinking of the scolding he'd get from Obaasan, the cleaner.

The concerto movement was finished. The student looked expectant. Dr Suzuki was still occupied with his cigarette. Eventually he stood and approached the young violinist.

'When you hold the bow, little finger should be so,' he said, demonstrating the bow-hold.

He returned to his chair and again studiously attended to the cigarette. It was the end of a very expensive lesson.

### THE VISITOR IN JAPAN

I was part of the tuning team at a graduation concert in Tokyo and appeared to be the only foreigner in the place.

## At the Kaikan

There were about 3,000 violins to be tuned and I had a line of children in front of me waiting; a single line which stretched back a long, long way. Mine was the batch of children who would play Schumann's *The Two Grenadiers*. I was suddenly aware that after I'd tuned each child's violin, he or she was going to the end of another line to be tuned 'properly' by someone who looked Japanese.

During the performance I chose to wander amongst the audience. It was interesting seeing the reaction of Japanese parents as they listened to the music. I was on an upper tier of the hall when I was suddenly confronted by a row of guards. This terribly obvious foreigner had wandered close to where the royal family was seated.

As usual, Dr Suzuki accompanied the last item on the piano – it was always *Twinkle, Twinkle* at a concert such as this. Sometimes he added a "new" *Twinkle* variation. It was generally the same one.

I was confronted by armed guards one day in a park in Tokyo. I was too close to the royal palace. It took me a while to understand what the problem was. When speaking about the Emperor, one should use a special vocabulary, so the guards were describing my blunder to me in words I'd never ever heard before.

(At the end of WWII, the Emperor made his Jewel Voice Broadcast in formal, classical courtly Japanese that few ordinary people could comprehend.)

While walking up one of the mountains outside Kyoto, I came across a monastery close to the summit. As I approached, a monk emerged and asked me to come in for tea. I was served tea and mandarins (*mikan*).

(The correct way to eat a mikan is to peel it carefully so the skin comes off in one piece. Then you can reassemble it to look full of fruit when you've finish eating.)

We sat in silence except for the call of a turtledove in the forest. Then the monk wished me well and I started down the mountain.

It wasn't long before a fog came down, so thick I could only just see the edges of the road. The birds stopped their calling, my footsteps were completely muffled. I was walking in a white stillness when out of the mist came a monkey. He stood in front of me. I had some peanuts in my pocket and offered a couple. From the forest came a whole group of these quiet, gentle animals, each taking my peanuts courteously as they walked down beside me. Lower down, the fog began to disperse and the animals melted back into the trees. I realised they were used to humans, notably the monks further up the mountain.

Some time later I went on a guided tour to Monkey Island. We were warned that the animals were vicious and not to put our hands anywhere near them. The guide led us along a track with a tall wire fence either side. Caged behind the wire, monkeys snarled, screamed and bared their teeth while our guide poked at them with a pointed stick. They were the same variety of monkey I'd seen up the mountain a few weeks before.

There you have it: "Monkey is the son of his environment."

I went into a coffee shop and sat down to order. Next to my table was a big cage containing a very Australian-looking cockatoo; white feathers and yellow crest.

We regarded each other while I waited for my

*At the Kaikan*

coffee, then the bird sidled along its perch and looked at me closely.

'Hullo, Cocky,' I offered.

He looked at me, head one side, then the other. He moved as near to me as he could.

'*Ohayō,*' he said in his little cockatoo voice.

(Cocky is the son of his environment.)

## My Japanese Made in Australia

I took ten Melbourne youngsters and a teacher to Matsumoto Summer School. We arrived a week before the event so the students could have lessons from Dr Suzuki, attended Summer School classes for two weeks then went down to Osaka for lessons with Miss Nakajima.

(Miss Nakajima is one of Japan's finest Suzuki violin teachers. When Dr Suzuki, in his later years, injured his shoulder badly and couldn't play, he needed an assistant to demonstrate at lectures and workshops. It was one of Miss Nakajima's students, Yuriko Watanabe, who was chosen to fill the position.)

Suzuki's lessons, as always, were on tone quality. He worked with my Melbourne children on bow balance and the achievement of a ringing sound.

*Listen to vibrating string.*

Back in Melbourne I'd made a tape of the instructions students would hear in Japanese (watch your bow-hold, careful with your posture, etc.) They'd all studied it hard and managed well in the Summer School classes.

There was a concert every afternoon at one o'clock. The young Japanese performers were always neatly dressed in navy trousers or skirts, and white tops. Dr Suzuki suddenly asked my ten students and my daughter to perform. This we did, dirty knees and all. I was teacher, tour guide and interpreter; nurse when necessary. I managed to tidy ten heads of hair before we went on stage but didn't think to look at my little boys' knees.

The next day at five to one, Dr Suzuki approached me.

'Today,' he said. 'Australian children will dance the minuet.'

'Yes, well...' I gulped. 'Perhaps tomorrow?'

'Tomorrow then,' Suzuki agreed. 'Australian children will dance the minuet.'

It is fearfully hot and humid in Matsumoto in summer. That very warm, airless evening, the Melbourne students and an additional ten Japanese children worked hard at my version of what I hoped looked like a minuet. Two of Miss Mori's students agreed to play Beethoven's *Minuet in G* for us.

At five to one the next day, Dr Suzuki came to me and said he wanted it danced fast. He sat at the piano and proceeded to play Beethoven at breakneck speed.

'Help!' I panicked to myself, but answered quietly that my students may not be able to dance at that speed. I asked a teacher to tell Dr Suzuki that a minuet maybe wouldn't be performed as fast as he'd just been playing.

The time came for our performance. We were all set to go, when Suzuki called out from the back of the hall.

'Please explain about a minuet.'

Right! I have about 800 Japanese parents, children and teachers, all eagerly watching and agog to see

## At the Kaikan

a demonstration of the dance. I was lucky. The day before, we'd watched a film of a Suzuki convention in Munich. I reminded my audience of the hall they'd seen, of the chandeliers; I explained about the clothes which would be worn in the eighteenth century...

'Which century?' Suzuki interrupted from the back row.

'The eighteenth,' I answered.

'Ah!' called Suzuki very loudly. 'In the seventeenth century, the minuet was fast.'

I was going well with my descriptions and explanations till I got to the word "wig". What the devil was the Japanese for "wig"?

'Excuse me,' I said through the microphone. I went to the side of the stage and explained the word I needed to one of the teachers.

'*Kaburi-mono,*' she whispered. The word didn't sound a bit familiar to me and I was sure I'd come across the word for "wig" before.

Never mind. I continued my explanation of eighteenth century silk and lace, buckled shoes, kaburi-mono, champagne... Everyone listened with rapt attention, fascinated to learn about the history of western culture.

We danced our minuet.

A few days later we visited a museum. The guide was showing us a suit of samurai armour and naming all the parts. You've guessed it! I'd told all those music students, parents and teachers that the minuet was danced in headgear a samurai could have worn.

The word for wig is *katsura.* I knew that! However, if I'd said that, my audience would have pictured a black-haired Japanese-type wig. I couldn't really win.

*Memories of Dr Shinichi Suzuki*

It was ages before it dawned on me why Dr Suzuki thought we'd be able to dance a minuet. I'd run some summer schools in Melbourne and at one of these had a dance expert teaching students to dance the minuet. We also had Miss Nakajima and students from Japan at the time. No doubt they'd reported to Dr Suzuki that the Australians had danced that particular dance.

It's easy to make mistakes with a foreign language. I'm absolutely positive I made a lot and was completely unaware of the fact. Just the minute change of one sound can make a drastic difference to a sentence. When I said *kusai* instead of *kyūsai* I asked a mother whether her child was stinking, instead of discussing her daughter's age. And when I said *konyoku* instead of *konnyaku*, I was asking a perfectly respectable and respected Miss Nakajima whether she liked bathing with men, not whether she liked the purplish-grey vegetable root jelly stuff on the dining table.

(When Miss Nakajima was staying with me in Melbourne one time and I asked her what she wanted for lunch, she mistook the word "needles" for "noodles".)

Of course I wasn't the only one in Matsumoto making language mistakes. There was the shop selling "Flesh Eggs", the restaurant where the waiter produced a "Ladies' Luncheon Menu", whatever the time of day or the sex of the customer. Then there was the little old lady in the laundromat one night, her back bent from a lifetime of work in the rice fields. She was clearly nervous of me, even though she proudly had foreign writing on her laundry bag.

The old lady pulled her dirty clothes from a bag clearly marked in English: "Hot Sex. Catch a Lover."

I wondered what wily mind had provided *that* sentence for the bag manufacturer.

Cathy and I disgraced ourselves giggling one day in a music shop as we read the English titles of songs in a guitar book which included: *500 Miles from Home* and *Hang Down Your Head, Tom Dooley*. These titles don't read well if written: *500 Miles from Homes* and *Hand Down Your Head, Tom Dooley*. But it was the words of America's proud and famous *Battle Hymn of the Republic*, born during the American Civil War, which had us nearly rolling with mirth:

> 'Mine eyes have seen the glory of the coming of the Lord,
>
> He is frampling in the vineyard where the grapes of warth are stored,
>
> He has loothed the faithful lightning of His frerrible swift sword,
>
> And His fruth is marching on.'

I must mention that Dr Suzuki was very patient with the over-familiar form of Japanese used by foreigners. Japanese vocabulary has several levels of politeness and we should have used one which really showed our respect for our teacher. He was, after all, Suzuki *Sensei* (teacher, master, professor). For all my language study in Australia, I learned a lot of my Japanese by associating with young adult kenkyūsei who spoke casual Japanese and by talking to shop assistants etc in Matsumoto. Later in Melbourne, a Japanese friend told me I speak like a Matsumoto peasant.

In Japanese, "Good morning" is *Ohayō* pronounced something like "Ohio". Easy for a foreigner to remember. One morning, Dr Suzuki told me he'd been greeted about an hour earlier by an American visitor.

'Iowa, Dr Suzuki,' the man had said brightly.
I looked at Dr Suzuki's impish expression.
'And what did you reply?' I asked.
Suzuki chuckled, his eyes twinkling: 'Ah! I am polite. I tell him, "Iowa".'

## THE SPIRIT OF A CHILD

When it was time for me to graduate from the training course, Suzuki Sensei said my final recital should finish with the Bach *D Minor Unaccompanied Partita*. Now I was no longer so young and I doubted my energy level was equal to the programme he chose. The last movement of that Partita takes about fourteen minutes and the thought of ending with that didn't thrill me.

I told Suzuki. The concept of insufficient stamina was quite beyond him. It took a while for him to understand.

'You could sit down,' he said…

Lois with Melbourne students at Summer School in Matsumoto.

*At the Kaikan*

Dr Suzuki always calculated his age by adding the digits. So when he was 73 he said he was 7 + 3 = 10.

*If you have the spirit of a young child, you never age.*

'Turning into a child
On New Year's Day,
I'd like that.'
(Issa)

## Lessons

Suzuki Sensei sometimes trained a video camera on a kenkyūsei who could then watch himself on the screen as he played, making it easier to grasp what changes needed to occur in his technique.

The technical exercise section of my private lesson might begin with an instruction such as: 'Please play note up-bow then note down bow. Second note please play take elbow down, then elbow carry bow. Up-bow start lower part bow. Please try…'
    I'd try.
    'No!'
    Another try.
    'No!'
    If I didn't eventually get what he had in mind, I'd say so.
    'But you did well yesterday! You played Bach in Monday concert!'
    Oh! Silly me! *That* bit! Now I understand.
    Another try.
    'So!'
    Back to the cigarette.
    It's no use just being able to play; a teacher must know exactly which muscles are needed to get the

required result. I often tell my students they've just played a passage well and ask them what they did correctly, in the hope they'll remember and do it again at home.

One day I just couldn't get the effect he wanted.

'Here,' he said. 'Your bow has learned bad habits. Use mine.'

He handed me his bow made by the Englishman, James Tubbs.[60]

It was the most incredible bow and the most incredible experience! It was so immaculately balanced; I felt I could just put my arm to my side and the bow would continue to play by itself. Together with his Italian violin by Landolphi,[61] it was magical equipment.

Suzuki had his little shoulder pad glued onto the back of his beautifully varnished eighteenth century violin.

We usually play at A440 pitch. When we tune to the note "A" (the next one above the piano's Middle C), we produce sound waves/cycles which hit the ear drum at 440 vibrations per second. The faster the vibration, the higher the pitch. Sometimes Suzuki decided to use another pitch for the day.

'Today we tune to A444,' he might say.

That makes intonation very difficult; you have to listen hard.

Kenkyūsei had a group lesson every week. Suzuki conducted the sessions with fun and games, just as he would for children. Perhaps we had to play the Bach *Concerto in A Minor* whilst answering maths questions, the Japanese kenkyūsei in English and

---

[60] James Tubbs of London (1836 – 1921).
[61] Carlo Ferdinando Landolphi (1734 – 1787).

any foreigners in Japanese. We had to use the polite form of the Japanese verb "to be". The polite form of "it's 259", *nihyakugojūkyū de gozaimasu*, takes a lot of saying alongside fast Bach.

Or we'd have to go to the front of the class and draw several straight bows on the Kreisler Highway. If we were successful we earned a chocolate. The

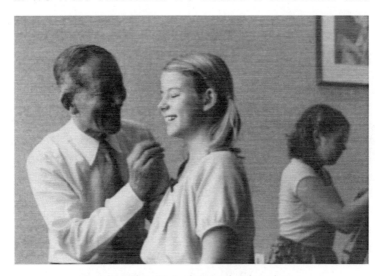

Lois's student Kate deserved a chocolate.

competition became quite fierce; it was good quality chocolate, not easily available in the shops. The kenkyūsei were thrilled when told, in Dr Suzuki's version of English: 'Now you become chocolate.'

Then he'd attempt the same task. As he grew older his bow was every which-way down the fingerboard. But you know what? With his equipment and the sensitivity of his bow arm, the sound was still beautiful.

'I become chocolate?' he'd ask hopefully.

'Oh yes, undeniably!'

Of course he always advocated working with the

upside-down bow. Practising holding the tip of the bow, with the frog in the air (we usually hold it at the frog end) is invaluable. We use this tactic to assist with the training of tone production. And if the bow feels out of balance in a certain part of a piece when upside down, it's an indication that it's out of balance at that same place when it's the right way up.

Our sensei always managed to remember the English words "upside down". But he never could remember "right way up".

'And now,' he'd falter. 'Another side.'

One of his games was to play a few notes from the middle of any piece – Violin Bk 1 to Bk 10 – and we had to play its beginning. We had to quickly work out which piece contained those few notes.

Sometimes he chose to do this when demonstrating his teaching methods to visitors. Then he'd look round the hall and choose who to bring on stage to be a guinea pig. As often as not it was me or Cathy, probably because our blonde hair was very obvious from a distance.

The art of being a musician is to think at speed. It is this quickness that teachers try to nurture in our students, the ability to "catch", to act on intuition.

*You can catch something.*

'Trying to catch
The lightning bolt
A child.'

(Issa)

During his lessons, Suzuki's agile mind and his lightness of touch kept both trainees and children alert.

> *Children learn abilities best when they are having fun.*

Fun and games certainly help keep a child alert but, inevitably, there have been teachers who observed his games and thought fun was the main aim of a Suzuki lesson. The joy of achievement is also fun!

Suzuki returned from a trip overseas and told us he'd observed a piano students' concert where all the performers' eyes were glued to their music and no one played at all sensitively.

'So,' he said. 'They can type...'

An American teacher brought a boy to Matsumoto. I think I remember it was his son. The gangling lad of about fourteen came glumly into the studio for a lesson. He played a piece from Bk 2 or 3. It was awkward, laboured playing. He was uncoordinated, out of tune, short of confidence and entirely unaware that he should be making a nice sound. It was really bad! Dr Suzuki looked startled as the boy began to play, then sat back in his chair and observed solemnly.

The rule is that when a Suzuki teacher or parent hears a student play, he should always congratulate/praise first and then offer constructive criticism. I wondered what on earth Dr Suzuki could possibly say to this poor boy.

Suzuki sat ignoring his cigarette, dazed by the performance. When the lad finished, our sensei jumped to his feet with alacrity.

'Good!' he said brightly and enthusiastically. 'You finished the piece!'

*Memories of Dr Shinichi Suzuki*

The boy's playing was rather better and he looked somewhat happier by the end of the lesson.

*Student must become better than teacher; if not is teacher's mistake.*

A kenkyūsei was having trouble controlling his bow. (The bow stick is very sensitive to any tremors in the hand or arm of the player)

'Sensei,' he said. 'My bow keeps jumping.'

Suzuki leapt from his chair, took the lad's bow and laid it on a shelf.

'Let me see,' he said excitedly as he watched it closely and for a long time. 'Let me see, let me see so wonderful a bow...'

He hated any hint of definition, any slight accent at the beginning of a note. 'I hear noise!' he'd complain.

I actually teach that "start". It's like the "t" sound made by the tongue at the beginning of a note on a wind instrument. For sure, it's not for all notes; it's dependant on the interpretation of the piece. Dr Suzuki hated the sound.

He used to say that William Primrose[62] was the last of the great string players. William was the renowned viola player for whom several composers, including Bartok, wrote concertos.

William and Suzuki argued about violin technique. Suzuki insisted one always held the instrument with the chin[63] and William insisted it wasn't necessary.

In fact it isn't always necessary but the technique has to be taught to beginners, ready for the time they'll need it. When changing the left hand position from a low note on any string (where the arm is

---

[62] Scottish viola player (1904 – 1982).

[63] Held firmly between the jaw and the left shoulder.

## At the Kaikan

extended away from you) to a higher note position (bringing the hand toward your shoulder), the move just throws the violin into your neck. Going back the other way, you can feel you are about to lose the fiddle. That's when you momentarily hold the instrument with the chin.

William used to do a brief flip up with his shoulder at this point to support the instrument – quite a difficult technique and not one I'd ever advocate.

They enjoyed their argument.

William's wife, Hiroko, was a Suzuki violin teacher, and a friend of mine. I remember her words as she opened a teacher training session at the NSW Conservatorium, 'First you must love little children.'

I chose to include the Mozart *Sonata KV378* in my graduation recital and realised the day before the event that I hadn't ever played it to my teacher. I thought I'd run the third movement at that day's lesson.

There's a big section in that piece that really needs to be played *spiccato* (a bow-bouncing staccato technique) and I'd been doing that. But I thought how Dr Suzuki didn't really teach off-string bowing much and decided to play it on the string for the lesson. I thought I'd just do spiccato at the concert.

There was an audience of American teachers in the studio as I fronted up for my lesson that day. Sensei stopped me after a few bars of the passage in question. He led me through the steps to acquire a flexible spiccato.

'Please try,' he said.

I repeated the passage as I'd preferred to do in the first place. Suzuki gave me a knowing look then turned to the American observers.

'Now she can do,' he said.

He flopped back into his chair and occupied himself with his cigarette.

I had inadvertently given him the opportunity to demonstrate how to teach the spiccato technique and hoped those teachers didn't think their own students would acquire it in about four minutes flat as I had appeared to do

Dr Suzuki had the most flexible fingers I've ever seen on any violinist. I'm not sure why he didn't teach this flexibility more frequently. I learned often to do as he did, but hadn't necessarily said.

Though at an advanced age he had supple fingers, his long thumb became straight or curved away from the bow hair. That's the opposite direction from what he advocated and everyone teaches. So I don't know how he managed his tremendous finger flexibility. It would appear to me to be defying the laws of nature…

### GO AND PRACTISE!

I finished my graduation recital with some contemporary pieces by Hasegawa. Suzuki called out from the audience asking me to play them again. He came to me at the end of the concert.

'I am so ashamed,' he said. 'I am so busy teaching Mozart and Beethoven, I forgot to look at modern Japanese music.'

*Suzuki* thought he should be *ashamed*?!

Very few older foreign teachers graduated from the course in Matsumoto. My final recital was big deal. I read my pledge to the children of the world; my calligraphy was hanging on stage behind me; a couple of my Japanese teacher friends had come to Matsumoto to hear me play.

I had practised my calligraphy for weeks to get it just the right style and was to sign it *Roisu* (Lois). I'd practised that too. A few days before I was to paint my final hanging, a kenkyūsei showed me how to write the Chinese kanji for "Fine silk gauze" and "Crossing the rapids". In Japanese, apparently, that was *roisu sepato*. The girl said that the kanji she suggested were close enough to *roisu shiepaado* (Lois Shepheard). When I showed Dr Suzuki my beautifully practised calligraphy with a scrawled, unpractised signature he was highly amused.

The day after my recital, I had my final lesson; I would go to the station straight after it and proceed to the airport.

'Please play first part Bach's *A Minor Concerto*, 2nd Movement,' said Suzuki.

'Now play same thing, first all *forte*, then all *piano*,' he instructed.

I complied and thought I did rather well.

'Oh, go back to Australia and practise!' he laughed with a dismissive wave of the hand.

I found out many years later that he always did that to departing graduates. We're never to think we know it all.

> *This is what I have learnt*
>
> *All the year I take care to change my tone; again I think it's a new sound. So, I believe in my heart that here indeed is the true string sound.*
>
> *How many times has this dream recurred!*
>
> *Now again I'm thinking about the new found natural sound.*

*Memories of Dr Shinichi Suzuki*

> *There again I heard a new singing string sound*
> *A journey of 30 years*
> *From here again I'm making a start*
> *Now, again throughout the year I am wide-eyed*
> *Here indeed is the true beautiful sound*
> *My foolish ears. Some sort of foolish person.*[64]

Suzuki Sensei gave me a framed painting he'd done of the Japan Alps. It has written on it:

> *Life in a beautiful sound.*

And he'd painted two of those long hangings with the beautiful calligraphy.

> *Man is the son of his environment.*
> *If love is deep, much can be accomplished.*

On the second of these, he wrote the translation in pen and ink in English, below the Japanese, and signed it in European script. The writing done with brush and a stick of Japanese ink is still perfectly clear but I've had to run over the English with a pencil before it faded away completely. I had to do the same with the English signature on my graduation certificate.

The word *shibui* can mean either tasteful and refined or so astringent as to pucker the mouth, depending on the Chinese character used. After my graduation recital, some kenkyūsei gave me a card, written in English, thanking me for a "puckering concert".

Dr and Mrs Suzuki were keen for me to teach

---

[64] *A Philosophy of Performance – 30 Years' Mediation on Sound.* (Shinichi Suzuki).

*At the Kaikan*

permanently in Japan. Mrs Suzuki was particularly anxious that I should stay. The town of Kurashiki in Okayama Prefecture needed a teacher.

Of course my family was in Australia so such a thought was out of the question. Also, I'd introduced the Suzuki Method to Victoria and made my repeated study visits to Japan for the benefit of my Melbourne teaching.

I did go down to Kurashiki to look round though. It was an interesting area, one of the few with foreign contact during the time of Japan's isolation. The buildings and canals are reminiscent of Holland – the influence of early Dutch traders.

## 11

## NURTURED BY LOVE

I still remember the night I left Japan after graduating from the Talent Education School of Music. Despite the fact that I was returning to my family in Australia, my departure was heartbreaking. Even now I remember the anguish.

Dr Suzuki was committed to educating the whole person. He taught us to play and teach the violin but quietly demonstrated the other qualities necessary to a teacher. He knew us as people, he understood our personalities, knew when we were upset or homesick, knew which of us took the time to study Japanese, who was short of money. He looked in on calligraphy classes, particularly the foreigners painting Japanese script for the first time. He continually kept an eye on us all. I think it wasn't till my plane was taking off from Tokyo Airport that I realised the extent of Dr Suzuki's concern for his students. We kenkyūsei had indeed lived in an environment where we were "nurtured by love".

## 12

## LATER YEARS

In Melbourne, my students played a concert with the Third District Army Band, resplendent in their red uniforms. Very good public relations for all concerned. I arranged a Seitz concerto and *The Two Grenadiers* for band accompaniment and we played *Twinkle, Twinkle* together with a full set of percussion and some Spanish rhythm variations to boot. I took a recording of the performance to Matsumoto.

'Too much percussion,' said Dr Suzuki.

With the pottery violin presented to him at the RVIB.

I had a student, a Vietnamese war orphan with both legs in callipers. When I started teaching him, I had him sit down to play but when he went to his first group lesson and found all the other children were standing he decided to do the same. It was a great accomplishment for that boy to balance on unsteady legs and wield something with his arms. His picture appeared in one of Melbourne's papers and I took a copy to show Dr Suzuki. He insisted that the boy's posture was very poor. As I showed him, his wife was with him.

'Ach, Suzuki,' she said. 'Can't you see he can't stand normally?'

For Dr Suzuki there was never a reason for a violinist to be satisfied with less than perfect. I'm sure he didn't appreciate what problems the little boy had.

Dr and Mrs Suzuki visited my students at the Royal Victorian Institute for the Blind (RVIB) School. Dr Suzuki happily posed with a nearly blind, partially deaf child with severe learning difficulties but he complained about her bow-hold after she played.

'Oh, Suzuki!' exclaimed his wife.

I met that girl some fifteen years later. She'd lost her sight altogether, was living in a hostel and working in a sheltered workshop. She came to me for a few more lessons. She said her family had given her an adult size violin for her 21$^{st}$ birthday and she'd continued playing, in her room at night, all those years without a teacher. I asked the young woman what she'd practised, picturing her there in the dark, enjoying her music.

'Dr Suzuki's *Twinkle, Twinkle*,' she answered.

I could have wept…

*Later Years*

One of the RVIB children gave Dr Suzuki a little stylised pottery, two pegged violin, made by his father a well known potter. Back in Matsumoto, Suzuki had a hoard of gifts presented to him from all round the world. They were politely received at the time then hidden forever down in the storeroom. The pottery violin, however, held pride of place and lived forevermore in his teaching studio.

Suzuki gave me a tape of a Japanese, totally blind piano student playing Beethoven. Wonderful playing.

In 1987 I took a group of Melbourne students to the International Suzuki Conference in Berlin. I'd been asked to give a lecture on teaching visually impaired pupils and the project grew from there. I decided to take some blind children and it dawned on me I'd need sighted children to take them to the

Dr Suzuki, Melbourne piano teacher Nehama Patkin, Lois, Mrs Waltraud Suzuki.

bathrooms. Eventually it was a chamber orchestra that left for Berlin and continued for appearances in Utrecht (Netherlands) and London.

In Berlin we played a couple of concerts, one in association with Melbourne piano teacher, Nehama Patkin and her students. In addition, Dr Suzuki asked if my group could play at one of his lectures. He cried during their performance of some Telemann.

After the lecture, my visually impaired students had their picture taken with him. They were aged thirteen to fifteen, all tall lads, around the 175 centimetre mark. Suzuki was a very small man, maybe 152 centimetres. Standing amongst my students he looked really diminutive. He caught my attention and beckoned. I went over and he pointed down to his feet. Shinichi Suzuki was up on his toes, straining his body to be as tall as he could be.

The leader of the orchestra was a highly intelligent lad of fifteen who had lost both eyes to cancer by the age of five.

Those readers who understand the violin know that a player turns his head slightly to the left. The left arm and the instrument are therefore somewhat out to the left, giving the right arm freedom to manipulate the bow. The longer the player's arms, the more room he needs for the bow arm. In that case his left arm needs to be taken out even further.

People without sight, however, aren't accustomed to turning their heads. Usually we turn our heads only to see something. I never did get the leader of my orchestra to turn his head and he grew to be enormously tall with extremely long arms. His technique was therefore cramped but he managed to play well; he performed a solo at the Berlin conference.

*Later Years*

Dr Suzuki was very impressed with him.

'You'll soon be playing the Tchaikowsky *Konzert*,' he said. (He always used the German word for "concerto".)

I delivered the lecture on teaching blind children and two of my lads again played solos. I had with me a therapist's assessment report on each child. According to that, one totally blind boy also suffered from autism. The report said he had no sense of direction, that if he took his hand off something he wouldn't be able to find the object again; it said he couldn't put toothpaste on a toothbrush. The boy then played Corelli's *La Folia* with all its sweeping chords requiring the bow to be lifted and replaced accurately on the strings.

*Every child can be educated.*

Years before, I'd watched a teacher taking group lessons in Matsumoto and the class included a lad with some type of intellectual disability. Each time his teacher announced the next piece to be played, the boy would come to the front of the stage, look down at me and ask if he knew it. I presume he chose me because of some fascination with my blonde hair. When I replied each time that he probably knew the work, he'd return to his group and happily play it. He managed many pieces but just couldn't remember their names. In Berlin in 1987 I noticed him in the class of the most advanced students, playing the Tchaikowsky *Concerto*.

As Suzuki said, any child who can speak his mother tongue can be taught to play an instrument. I have found, in fact, that a child who cannot speak can still be taught to play the violin.

I've had some students who only repeat what is said to them (echolalic) and not able to think up a new conversation, or topic of conversation. These children can be taught to copy a CD exactly but won't be able to devise some interpretation of their own.

That, ultimately, is the aim of a musician. Suzuki would become quite excited when a kenkyūsei displayed certain flair and ideas of his own.

'Ah! He understands!'

I've taught students with the ability to say the occasional word if prompted but actually with no verbal communication. They can be taught to play. Their violin performance can even flow and be fairly accurate even though there may be minimal understanding. There is obvious enjoyment.

Dr Suzuki with a visually impaired child in Melbourne.

*Later Years*

During a return visit to Japan, I was teaching a class of little children to play Handel's *Bourrée*. In the course of the lesson, I had them turn their backs to me and copy what I played. I gradually moved from a *Twinkle* rhythm to "Waltzing Matilda". I often have fun with that. The mothers in the room obviously knew the Australian tune and asked me to tell them about the words. I began to translate it for them.

As I related about someone stealing sheep and jumping into a water hole and a ghost calling out an invitation to join him, I noticed those mothers looked very confused. Suddenly it hit me what the problem was.

'This is not our National Anthem,' I said. 'It's a folk song.'

Much relief, smiling and nodding…

As he grew older, Dr Suzuki went deaf and he began to demand more and more sound from his students. I was glad I studied with him when I did, when he could still discern a good sound.

'Play to Suzuki bad ear,' he started to say.

The resulting sound from his kenkyūsei became very forced and insensitive. Gradually, Suzuki's only teaching technique became the upside-down bow for the training of a loud sound.

Once, back in Melbourne, I was leading a huge group of children playing the Lully *Gavotte* at a concert in the presence of Dr and Mrs Suzuki. When we started with the first two up-beat crotchets, the accompanist mistook the piece for one of those that then proceeds much faster and set off at a gallop. The children followed the piano, not me.

I was very embarrassed! This in front of Dr Suzuki! I chose to repeat the piece (other Melbourne teachers were shocked that I did this). A teacher crawled across the stage amongst the sea of violinists and told the accompanist to watch me this time. We set off. The same thing happened.

Of course it's interesting that the children had the technique to play at near double speed.

Dr Suzuki thought the whole thing was wonderfully entertaining.

That concert was at the Dallas Brookes Hall and it was in that same venue a few years later that Suzuki slipped on the floor in the gentlemen's toilet and injured his left shoulder very badly. He was by now very old and the fall had a great impact on his ability to play and teach.

After that I saw him in the United States on a few occasions and though he was still mentally alert, his shoulder definitely gave him trouble.

I saw Dr Suzuki for the last time about 1990. My daughter returned to Matsumoto a year or two after that and reported that he was still teaching, though with less success. After Takao Mizushima of Sydney revisited him later in the 1990s he told me, 'Dr Suzuki is just resting.'

Shinichi Suzuki passed away on the 26$^{th}$ of January, 1998 aged 99.

I was at my holiday house in South Gippsland. It was a very hot morning. I looked out through the glass door as I answered the phone, noting the light wind blowing the very long, dry grass. It was potential bush fire weather, I was called to attention by my friend's voice. She told me Suzuki was gone.

It was a terrible moment.

*Finale*

The master we all loved so much was no more. The man who gave himself to the search for "love, truth, virtue and beauty" was no longer with us. The teacher who spent a lifetime following the sound of Kreisler and Casals was at rest.

Shortly afterwards, a Melbourne teacher asked me if I thought the "Suzuki Tone" quality would undergo a change. Of course sound changes! Suzuki's sound and his tonal effects were ever changing; the legacy he left us was the task of researching sound production and teaching it to children.

> *I was a lone traveller on a journey in the search for sound... My efforts have extended the boundaries of my mental capacity.*

# 13

# FINALE

Dr Suzuki with Lois's students Claire and Justine.

I hope this selection of memories has given you an idea of the man who gave careers to tens of thousands of Suzuki teachers and joy to millions of children and their parents.

*Character first, ability second.*

The above quote was the motto of the commercial school Suzuki attended as a young man. He adopted it as one of his own; it so aptly described his view on education.

*I respect all living things.*
*Do not hurt anybody's heart.*
*What is man's ultimate aim in life?*
*It is to look for love, truth, virtue and beauty.*

Despite his wish to produce people with fine character – music lovers, not professionals – he filled music studios with outstanding teachers and the symphony orchestras of the world with capable players. Of course he has filled concert halls with more knowledgeable listeners.

When I first introduced the Suzuki Method to Melbourne, I received a lot of publicity and was asked to speak to parent groups, music teachers, kindergartens etc. Some people came just to argue. Music teachers didn't want to accept the fact that talent wasn't hereditary and they certainly didn't want to hear about something from Japan. Sometimes a member of the audience would throw the whole Japanese prison camp story at me.

The notion of a recording of pieces to be learned was considered revolutionary.

'I can't see why the teacher can't demonstrate in the lessons,' they argued.

'Maybe because not a lot of teachers can play like Kreisler,' I answered.

Nowadays, there's a CD with practically every music instruction book for any instrument, be it the classics, jazz or whatever.

I was asked how it was that musicians such as Mozart learned without access to recordings. Of course, those great musicians of long ago grew up surrounded by music.

> *Outstanding musicians like Bach, Beethoven and Mozart were all raised in outstanding musical environments, and went through physiological adaptations in the areas of intelligence, sensibility, and music.*

Nor could teachers understand the idea that a child should be taught to play first and read music later. Even today, the old criticism occasionally raises its ugly head - that students of the Suzuki Method aren't taught to read! Years ago, one of my students performed the Mendelssohn *Concerto* for an audition. The auditor asked her if she could read music. What a wondrous ability a student would have if he or she could learn such a complex piece with no reference at all to a written score!

And how ludicrous it would be to ask a little child to read his mother tongue before he tried to utter a word. Furthermore, before the age of about seven, the average child's eyes have difficulty tracking sideways as is necessary when reading music. So the reading process needs to be delayed till about that age. At seven, many Suzuki students are already very advanced players.

In Japan, the Ministry of Education (*Monbusho*) has a well planned music programme for all schools. The course outline I have from years ago shows that Grade One children had the same number of music lessons as they had maths. I acquired a set of school music books; the ones for elementary school show there is instruction in reading and playing percussion and keyboard instruments from Grades One and Two. The reading books Dr Suzuki produced were primarily to help Suzuki parents.

When I first introduced the Suzuki Method to

*Finale*

Victoria, I was concerned that teachers and parents mightn't understand it. I voiced these concerns to a teacher friend[65] and we rationalised that if teachers used any facet of Dr Suzuki's teaching, whether the positive approach, the search for a beautiful sound, the parental assistance or the pieces in the well planned violin instruction books with the reference recordings, they would probably do better than they had done before.

I startled Melbourne's music teachers with that first batch of Suzuki students. Till then, only about half a dozen teachers taught primary age beginners. The bulk of violin students in Victorian government schools were in the Technical Schools and began learning at the age of fourteen.

A friend asked me recently how it is that I remember my time with Dr Suzuki so vividly. Suzuki's charisma, his gentle warmth, his unvarying friendliness would be hard to forget. When I began writing this book, many memories were well to the fore. As I continued and revised, my mind released many more. Some recollections bring me a deep sadness that his physical presence is no longer with us. I'm grateful for the time I spent with him and happy that I can try to continue his work with children and music.

Musicians, educators and politicians applauded Suzuki in Japan and abroad. Illustrious concert artists went to Japan and paid homage to the man who spent his life guiding students towards the sound of Kreisler and Casals. Visitors to Matsumoto

---

[65] Peter Komlos in Hobart – Pioneer of the Suzuki Method in Australia

included such as violinists Yehudi Menuhin[66] and David Oistrakh[67] and flautist Marcel Moyse.[68] But surely for Dr Suzuki, the ultimate joy would have been the visit of the great cellist Pablo Casals himself in 1961. The maestro was entertained at a concert by violinist and cellist children.

Suzuki gave me a tape of the concert and Casals' speech (in English). Through his tears the great cellist congratulated the teachers and parents saying how wonderful it was to see grown up people thinking of the smallest and teaching them "noble feelings" and "noble deeds" such as music.

He continued, 'Music is not only sound to have to dance or to have small pleasure, but such a high thing in life that perhaps it is music that will save the world.'

We can't even begin to imagine Dr Suzuki's sentiments as he listened to Pablo Casals' conclusion:

> 'Japan is a great people. And Japan is not only great with its deeds, in industrial [sic], in science, in art but Japan is, I would say, the heart of the heart and this is what humanity needs, first, first, first.'

Somewhere in the audience, a sixteenth size violinist practised the note 'E' with the first rhythm of *Twinkle, Twinkle*.

Some Japanese teachers who visited Dr Suzuki in Matsumoto knelt and bowed with their foreheads to the floor. I am mentally doing the same, as I remember the remarkable, brilliant, sweet natured,

---

[66] Yehudi Menuhin, born in New York (1916 – 1999).
[67] Russian, David Oistrakh (1908 – 1974).
[68] Marcel Moyse, France (1889 – 1984)

childlike, never tiring, straightforward, deep thinking, earnest, patient, intuitive, generous and humble gentleman who happily and quietly turned the music education world upside down.

I bow again.

Lois's graduation.

## Coda

I wrote this book with members of the "Suzuki world" in mind. However, it may well take the interest of a reader with no contact with the Suzuki Method. I offer you this very brief sketch:

The Suzuki Method teacher always remembers that 'every child can be educated', the quality of that education depending on the child's particular environment – both at home and in the teaching studio.

The Foreword in the new (2007) international edition of the *Suzuki Violin School, Volume 1*[69] begins with an excerpt from Dr Suzuki's writing and includes a plea to Suzuki parents:

*Please raise your child to be a fine human being.*

Weekly instrumental lessons are taken individually and there are periodic lessons in a class.

Parents attend all lessons, help the child as he practises at home and also learn to play the instrument to a very elementary level so as to grasp the basics of the technique.

The reference recording is played at home daily. Suzuki advocated twice as much listening time as practice time. Children are hearing the <u>language</u> of music just as they hear the mother tongue. The music is learned by ear until the child has settled into some technical proficiency; not before the age of <u>about seven.</u> In the early stages, the printed copy is

[69] Summy-Birchard Inc. Print rights administered by Alfred Publishing Co. Inc.

for the parent.

Taking his cue from the medicine bottle, Suzuki recommended that very young children should practise for:

*Two minutes with love, five times per day.*

The music in the instruction books was meticulously selected. Apparently it took some ten years of trial and error before Dr Suzuki was satisfied with Violin Book 1. Material in the books for other instruments has been selected with the same care by various authors.

As each piece introduces a new technique, it reinforces previously learned material. After all, when a child is learning its mother tongue, we don't declare: 'Don't say "dog". You said that yesterday.' For the same reason, previously learned pieces are revised. The periodic class sessions help considerably in the revision process.

The teacher always pays close attention to the child's developing tone quality. As you will realise, this concentration on sound is an integral part of the method. There will be adjustments to technique to assist the tonal development, the teacher remembering to compliment the student on something or other, before suggesting a change. We are using the instrument and music to cultivate a child's self esteem, sensitivity, concentration etc. and we handle each lesson accordingly. The responsibility of helping to shape the mind of a child is tremendous.

*When the human race created the culture of speech and writing,*

*it also produced the sublime culture called music.*

*It is a language that goes beyond speech and letters*

*– a living art that is almost mystical.*

Dr Suzuki with little Rosie. Photograph courtesy of *The Age*.

## Acknowledgements

***Front Cover:*** Image of Dr Suzuki, courtesy of TERI, Matsumoto

***Back Cover:*** Japanese script, painted by Dr Suzuki, says Man is the Son of His Environment. Violin image: iStockphoto.com

***Jacket Design:*** David P Reiter

Two of my friends urged me to write my memories of Dr Suzuki. They are Vilma Dyball, former Suzuki parent and now the mother of three professional musicians; Justine Clark, my former student, now a Suzuki teacher. Vilma kindly wrote the blurb for the back cover. Thank you both for your continued interest.

I wish to thank Mitsuko Kawakami, Secretary to the President at the Talent Education Research Institute, Matsumoto, Japan, for her willing assistance. Thank you to Lesley Priest, Marjorie Hystek and Anne Lewis for additional reminiscences.

I feel sure Dr Suzuki would have been happy with the way his teaching method has developed in Victoria where our teachers, teacher-trainers, members of the various committees, Suzuki students and their parents do their utmost to follow his principles. They are all to be congratulated.